Colin Davies

THINKING ABOUT ARCHITECTURE

An Introduction to Architectural Theory

Laurence King Publishing

PICTURE CREDITS

THINKING ABOUT ARCHITECTURE

An Introduction to Architectural Theory

Published in 2011
by Laurence King Publishing Ltd
361–373 City Road
London EC1V 1LR
Tel: +44 (0)20 7841 6900
Fax: +44 (0)20 7841 6910
E-mail: enquiries@laurenceking.com
www.laurenceking.com

A catalogue record for this book is available
from the British Library

ISBN 978 185669 755 2

Designed by Draught Associates

Printed in China

CONTENTS

INTRODUCTION

In the 1950s, architectural theory in Europe and America was a makeshift affair, a mixture of old ideas about composition surviving from the time when architecture students were expected to know about the classical orders, newer ideas about form and function derived from the modernist manifestos of the 1910s and 20s, and a body of research aimed at making the process of design more rational and scientific. The discipline was intellectually rather un-ambitious.[1] Theory stuck close to practice, which seemed the only way to justify its existence. By the mid 1960s those modernist ideas had become an orthodoxy and were already beginning to seem a little stale. Teachers and writers on the fringe of the profession began to ask if architecture really was just about problem solving and the updating of the building industry. In Italy, for example, Aldo Rossi sought to restore respect for the pre-modern European city in his book *L'architettura della città,* first published in 1966 (published in English as *The Architecture of the City* in 1982) and Manfredo Tafuri brought Marxist theory to bear on architecture in his book *Progetto e Utopia*, first published in 1973 (published in English as *Architecture and Utopia* in 1976). Meanwhile, in America, Robert Venturi's *Complexity and Contradiction in Architecture* (1966) laid the foundation for a new post-modernist critique, and the MIT-based magazine *Oppositions* began to publish decidedly intellectual articles by architect/thinkers like Peter Eisenman, Colin Rowe and Alan Colquhoun.

   Two distinct philosophical strands began to emerge: a phenomenological approach, typified by the popularity among architects, teachers and students of a book called *The Poetics of Space* by the French philosopher Gaston Bachelard, and the revival of an old idea: that architecture might be thought of as a kind of language. At about this time, controversy was raging in the English departments of universities about a new approach to literary criticism that went by the name of Structuralism. Structuralism came from France and before long French

An illustration from Aldo Rossi's *La città analoga* (1976). The collage of layered images is analogous to the layered history of the city.

critical theory, represented by thinkers such as Claude Lévi-Strauss, Michel Foucault, Roland Barthes and Jacques Derrida, began to spill over into the relatively much smaller cultural field of architectural theory. Suddenly it seemed possible that architectural theory might become more than just an adjunct to the practice of architectural design; with an injection of French critical theory, it might become a respectable branch of philosophy in its own right. It was not long before post-graduate courses in the new architectural theory were being set up in British and American universities.[2] People began to specialize in it and not all of them were architects. The link between practice and theory weakened. Theory was now seen mainly as a form of criticism, not just of individual buildings but of the city as a whole and of the relationship between architecture and modern life. It began to float free, developing its own language, its own kind of writing, its own store of ideas. It became a kind of miniature economy, producing books, articles and paper projects for consumption by a small group of specialist post-graduate students who then went on to produce more books, articles and paper projects.

A self-contained speciality

Architectural theory in this new form was not meant for architects and architectural educators, or even for architectural critics in the everyday sense, still less for non-professionals with an interest in, and love of, architecture. It was meant for other architectural theorists. Was there anything wrong with this? Perhaps not. The pursuit of theory for its own sake brought intellectual rewards that a less rigorous and penetrating approach might have failed to reach. But theory had become a self-contained speciality and the difficulty of penetrating it, of learning

its language and understanding its approach, meant that it failed
to inform the rest of the cultural field that we call architecture.
In schools of architecture, for example, where the main thrust of
the course is the project-based teaching of design, the teaching of
theory was either hived off into small, separate enclaves or taught
in a fragmentary way in occasional lectures and seminars which
went straight over the heads of the mostly practical and visually-
orientated students. There was simply not enough time to undertake
the necessary preparatory teaching in general philosophy. The new
theory effectively blocked the development of a different kind of
theory that might actually have served to strengthen and clarify the
thinking of practising designers.

Generally speaking this is still the situation. From the point
of view of most people who are interested in architecture, there are
four main problems with the discipline of architectural theory as
at present constituted. The first is the overvaluing of novelty. Like
most academic disciplines, architectural theory is competitive, and
the best way to compete is to come up with something new. In the
past this has often meant finding a French philosopher that nobody
else knows about. So just when we had got used to Structuralism
– the principles of Ferdinand de Saussure's linguistic analysis, for
example – along came the phenomenologists saying that we had to
read Maurice Merleau-Ponty and perhaps Martin Heidegger. Then
avant-garde architects like Bernard Tschumi and Peter Eisenman
found out about Jacques Derrida's Deconstruction (such a temptingly
architectural designation) and began to apply it to architecture. No
sooner had we got used to that idea (if we ever did) than everybody
was talking about Gilles Deleuze and the possible relevance to
architecture of, for example, his concept of 'the fold'. I do not
mean to imply, of course, that these were in any way regressive or
regrettable developments or that the breaking of new ground should
be discouraged. But the relentless, competitive forward motion of the
discipline soon left the non-specialist far behind. One philosopher
after another became fashionable and each was treated as if he or
she had all the answers.

The second problem is an emphasis on named philosophers
rather than on themes that might be useful to architects. If we want
some help understanding buildings, whether our own designs or
other people's, we do not want to immerse ourselves in the life's
work of a particular philosopher, very little of which is relevant to
the questions we actually have in our minds. Once again, I don't
want to discourage anybody from trying to fathom the depth of
thinking of Derrida or Deleuze, but such a project might be out of
proportion with the immediate need to understand or communicate
fundamental ideas about meaning in architecture or about the
relationship between design and natural processes. We should
reserve the right to learn from the philosophers without becoming
philosophers ourselves. A publisher recently launched a series of
books with titles like *Heidegger for Architects* and *Deleuze and
Guattari for Architects*[3], which is an excellent idea, but still requires
us to approach theory through specific philosophical channels, one

at a time, when what we really need is a thematic approach that focuses the philosophical ideas in areas that our own curiosity leads us to.

The third problem is the problem of obscurity. Some subjects are genuinely hard to understand and require special languages to handle their concepts. Quantum physics might be case in point. Is architectural theory difficult in this sense? Perhaps it is. But there might also be something else going on, something that is familiar in many fields of elite culture: the operation of a law of intellectual supply and demand. In order to maintain a position as an expert in any given field of culture, one needs to know things – ideas, theories, the contents of certain books – that almost nobody else knows. The smaller the number of people that know them, the more valuable they are. If everybody knows them, they are worth nothing. So it is a good idea to protect them and limit their circulation. Of course it is necessary for people to know *about* them, and to think that they are worth knowing, so complete secrecy would be self-defeating, but it is essential to maintain their market value. We are not necessarily talking about monetary value, though that may come into it indirectly. More often we are talking about intellectual authority and prestige. One way to control the supply of ideas is to make them hard to understand, to talk about them in a kind of code or special language that has to be learnt and practised. A lot of architectural theory is written in just such a language. Here is a typical example published in 1994 in the *Journal of Architectural Education*. It is the introduction to an article called 'Representation and Misrepresentations: On Architectural Theory'.

> 'A recent trend in architectural theory is the derivation of methodology from a post structuralist critique of representation to illuminate the triangulation of architectural production, representation, and power. Using an exemplary text by Mark Wigley, the article questions whether this (or any) theoretical endeavour is exempt from the attractions to power that it strives to disclose. It considers a contradiction characterized by a theory's shift of attention away from architecture's multiple claims toward the production of theory itself, and it illuminates the consequences of theoretical endeavours that avoid contact with resistencies put forth by non-discursive architectural thought.'[4]

The relentless abstractness of this kind of writing – all those shapeless Latinate words, piled one on top of another – make this a challenging read even for someone familiar with the style. And bear in mind that this is the introduction to the article, printed in bold print at the top of the page, where we might reasonably expect something more gentle and enticing. Note also that the article is based on an earlier article by Mark Wigley called 'The Production of Babel, the Translation of Architecture', which in turn is based on an article by Jacques Derrida called 'Architecture where the Desire May Live'. The main underlying idea is an important one – that philosophy often makes use of architecture as a metaphor and that this has interesting consequences for architectural theory. But we are very far removed from anything visible or tangible, anything recognizably architectural in the ordinary sense, like a building. Most readers, even if they know and understand a lot about architecture, will soon give up trying to understand this article. It is useless to architecture in the broad sense. The important thing to its writer, however, is that limiting its accessibility maintains its value in the limited market of architectural theory.

The fourth problem with architectural theory has already been touched upon: its increasing remoteness from practice. Theory and practice have effectively parted company. Theory is still taught in schools of architecture (where else would it find a home?) but mainly as a separate speciality. It is no longer contained within the disciplinary boundaries of architecture. Of course, breaking through disciplinary boundaries might be a good and necessary thing to do – a consequence of the age-old tension between structure and content, between the urge to be set free from things like disciplinary boundaries and the need to know where one stands and how to orientate oneself. But in this case, at this time, there is a need to restore a sense of balance, to re-establish a line of communication between theory and practice, to re-ground theory and prevent it from floating off into the intellectual stratosphere.

And that is what this book sets out to do. It does not reject the discoveries that theory has made over the past 40 years but absorbs them and links them with earlier theories, striving for clarity rather than novelty. Understanding has too often been blocked by theorists' refusal to meet architectural readers on their own territory. This book is addressed directly to architectural readers. It uses ordinary language, not specialist jargon, and it takes the trouble to explain things rather than taking for granted an unrealistic depth of understanding. It is organised thematically, not chronologically or biographically. It is neither a history of theory nor an introduction to named philosophers. Names are mentioned in passing and can be looked up in the footnotes and bibliography but the main focus is on ideas.

In order to begin to understand architecture in all its cultural complexity it is necessary to grasp certain basic concepts such as representation, typology, tectonics, the language metaphor, the organic metaphor, harmonic proportion and authorship. These and other concepts are introduced at the most basic level. Sometimes it is useful and illuminating to restate and see afresh the 'blindingly' obvious. But this is not a children's book and the development of those concepts at times leads to quite subtle and advanced interpretations, including many that are the product of recent architectural theory. Reading this book might be good way to break into that specialized, academic field but that is not its main aim. Its main aim is provide designers, teachers, students, and interested laypersons with a set of ideas that will enrich their conversation, their writing, and above all their thinking about architecture.

What is architecture?

But before we begin examining some of those basic concepts, we should first take an overview of the territory that we shall be exploring, the territory called 'architecture'. What is architecture? That must be the first question in any book about architectural theory. The dictionary tells us that the word means 'the design of buildings'.

Does this include all buildings or only some of them? The twentieth-century architectural historian Nikolaus Pevsner famously said that Lincoln Cathedral was a piece of architecture but that a bicycle shed was just a building. For him, a building had to be designed 'with a view to aesthetic appeal' before it could be called architecture. Those of us of an egalitarian frame of mind might wish to abolish this class distinction and extend the concept of architecture to include even the most humble structures. Surely even a bicycle shed can be beautiful? On the other hand, if all buildings are architecture, then the word ceases to mean much. We might as well just talk about buildings. It might be more useful to ask ourselves what the word 'architecture' actually refers to in practice, to list all of its meanings and connotations. If we do then we will find that, in the most general sense, it refers to a specialized cultural field in which certain kinds of people compete for social and cultural capital. This field includes not only architects and the work that they do, but everything else associated with architecture: its values, ideologies, specialized skills, jargon, codes of conduct, professional institutions, education, history, books, magazines, exhibitions, networks of patronage, prominent personalities, mythical heroes and canonical buildings. What it does not include, rather surprisingly, is most ordinary buildings. Popular housing, for example, which is probably the most common building type, is routinely excluded from architecture conceived as a cultural field. You will not find many developer-built suburban housing estates featured in architectural history books, magazines or exhibitions. The architecture field is not an abstract concept but a concrete social formation. It is therefore full of imperfections and absurdities and arguably is in need of radical reform. Such reform is not, however, among the aims of this book, which is content to inhabit the architecture field, describing its theoretical parts as accurately as possible in the hope that this might be helpful to future reformers.

The architecture field is a small branch of western culture. It nevertheless extends all over the developed world with outposts even in relatively remote non-western societies. That is not to say that it represents the only architectural tradition. China, Japan, India, the Middle East, Africa and pre-Columbian America all have rich architectural histories stretching back to ancient times. But it is the western tradition that has ridden the expansive wave of twentieth- and twenty-first-century globalization and for that reason the examples used in this book are mostly drawn from that tradition. In some cases this is an arbitrary choice, a bias resulting from the author's background and education. Often the examples might almost as easily have been chosen from non-western traditions, and in a few cases they have been – the Ise Shrine in Japan, for example, the Dravidian Hindu temples of southern India or the vernacular architecture of Morocco. But in other cases, such as the discussion of harmonic proportion, only western examples will do. Some might see this as an annoying inconsistency but this is a practical as well as a theoretical book. It does not aim to break new ground but to be a guide for newcomers to a territory already mapped out, and that territory, like history itself, is partial, biased and heterogeneous.

CHAPTER 1
REPRESENTATION

Consider the following quotation from the introduction to a book called *Architecture in the Age of Divided Representation* by Dalibor Vesely:

> 'In a conventional understanding, representation appears to be a secondary and derivative issue, associated closely with the role of the representational arts. However, a more careful consideration reveals, very often to our surprise, how critical and universal the problem of representation really is.'[1]

The passage goes on to develop the idea that architecture, like painting and sculpture, is a representational art. How can this be? Surely architecture is just the design of buildings, and the main function of most buildings is to provide shelter from the weather for a variety of human activities? Buildings are practical things, not so different from boats or bridges or umbrellas. How can a building represent anything in the way that, say, a portrait represents a person? What does architecture have to do with painting and sculpture? We have no difficulty with the idea that painting and sculpture are representational arts. Even an abstract painting seems to represent something, some intangible or hard-to-define aspect of experience, like an emotion or a predicament. Perhaps it is precisely because painting has no obvious practical function that we assign to it the function of representation. By the same token, architecture, because it does have an obvious practical function, ought surely to be relieved of the function of representation? So why do theorists insist that buildings often, or perhaps always, represent something beyond themselves? I have chosen ancient Greek temples to illustrate some possible answers to this question, for several reasons: because Greek temples are familiar and easy to visualize; because, being somewhat removed from our everyday experience, they have a certain simplicity and purity; and because they have so often been seen as the original prototypes of western architecture. But this is not a chapter *about* Greek temples. The arguments apply in principle to all architecture.

Sculpture and architecture

One obvious way that a building can be representational is when it incorporates painting or sculpture. A very famous ancient building will serve as an excellent example. The Panathenaic frieze is a long strip of shallow relief sculpture, originally painted, that was incorporated into the temple known as the Parthenon in Athens. It is thought to represent a procession that took place annually in the ancient city on the 'birthday' of the goddess Athena to whom the temple is dedicated. Most of the frieze was removed from the ruined building by Lord Elgin in the early nineteenth century and installed in the British Museum, but originally it was wrapped like a ribbon round the top of the 'cella', or enclosed part of the temple, behind the 'peristyle', or external colonnade. It was not added to the structure, like a painting hanging on a wall, but was carved *in-situ* out of stone of which the wall was built. It is therefore 'incorporated' in the true sense. And it is certainly representational. In fact it is considered to be one of the supreme examples of representational art in the whole western tradition. When it first arrived in London, John Flaxman, the outstanding English sculptor of the day, described it simply as 'the finest work of art I have ever seen'.[2]

But is it architecture? Surely it is just surface ornament and not in any way essential to the function of the building. This is true, though one might argue about what the true function of the building was exactly. After all, the goddess Athena did not really need to be sheltered from the weather. Perhaps the real function of the building was precisely to provide a frame for monumental sculpture, including the long lost ten metre (32.8 foot) high gold and ivory statue of the goddess that stood in the gloomy interior. Sculpture representing mythical scenes like the birth of Athena and her battle with Poseidon was literally framed by the gables or 'pediments' at either end of the roof. Elgin removed most of this sculpture too and looking at it close up in the museum, you can see how inventive the sculptor had to be to fit his figures into the awkward tapering space allotted to them. Evidently, the frame came before the figures. In other words architecture took precedence over sculpture. Besides, not all Greek temples were equipped with representational friezes and pediment sculptures, so we can't argue that these were essential components of temple architecture. We have to conclude that sculpture-framing was at best a secondary function of the building.

So far, then, architecture remains aloof from representation. But the sculpture is not the only artistic stonework in the Parthenon. More obviously 'functional' parts of the building such as columns, beams and roof overhangs, are also artistically carved, though in a more abstract way. The tops or 'capitals' of the columns, for example, take the form of flat plates sitting on exquisite swelling cushions of stone. In the upper part of the 'entablature' that rests on the columns, relief panels called 'metopes', depicting fights between lapiths and centaurs (many also removed by Elgin), alternate with 'triglyphs' embellished by abstract triangular grooves. So here representation and abstraction

The Parthenon, Athens – the classic three-quarter view from the Propylaea, or gateway, to the Acropolis. This is perhaps the most familiar image in the whole history of architecture and is therefore an appropriate starting point. Greek temples conveniently illustrate questions of representation.

A section of the Panathenaic frieze from the Parthenon. The gods Apollo, Artemis and Poseidon meet and converse in strikingly relaxed poses. The frieze, most of which is now in the British Museum, was carved *in-situ* into the upper part of the cella wall. Is it therefore an example of representation in architecture?

sit side by side. But the distinction is not as clear cut as it seems. Most archaeologists agree that the earliest Greek temples were made of wood and that the surviving stone structures preserve certain features of the old timber technology. The triglyphs are a case in point. They probably mark the positions of the original wooden roof beams. This means they are not really abstract at all because they *represent* a feature of the original construction. If we accept this, then we have to see the whole building as a piece of sculpture, a representation in stone of a wooden original. And those wooden temples, houses for gods, were representations of houses for tribal chieftains, which in turn were enhanced representations of houses for ordinary people. This is not quite the same kind of representation that we see in traditional figurative painting and sculpture. The building is representing something of its own kind – another building or itself in a former existence – not something of a different kind like a human figure or a landscape. Nevertheless, we seem to have found a way in which a whole building, not just its sculptural parts, can be said to be representational.

Triglyphs and metopes carved into the entablature of the Parthenon. The metopes represent mythical beings such as lapiths and centaurs, but the triglyphs are also representational. They stand for the ends of roof beams in the original wooden version of the temple.

Architectural history books are full of buildings that represent other buildings. We might even go so far as to say that representation in this simple sense is almost a universal characteristic of architecture. Architects in the west have for centuries copied ancient architectural details such as those we have seen in the Parthenon, and used them to ornament their own buildings. Walk down the old main street of almost any European or American city and you will see countless nineteenth- and twentieth-century versions of these details in the facades above the shop fronts. The long chain of representation – copies of copies of copies, each reinterpreting its model, sometimes altering the standard forms or combining them in new ways, sometimes returning to the pure originals – is called the classical tradition. The story of its development forms the greater part of the history of western architecture.

Columns and the human figure

Near the Parthenon, on the high plateau of the Acropolis, stands another ancient temple known as the Erechtheion. Here we can see an even clearer example of sculpture incorporated into architecture. A kind of plinth or rostrum, sheltered by a flat canopy, projects forward from the south wall of the temple, facing the Parthenon. The canopy is supported by 'caryatids' – columns in the shape of female human figures. So should we think of these columns as sculpture or architecture? They are

certainly not abstract or purely functional. In his treatise *De Architectura*, the ancient Roman architectural theorist Marcus Vitruvius Pollio tells us that caryatids represent the women captured by the Spartans when they sacked the city of Caria and killed all the men. We shouldn't take Vitruvius too literally. In the ancient world mythical and historical truth did not necessarily coincide and in any case the designation of these particular column figures as 'caryatids' is relatively recent. In the modern, archaeological sense, the 'true' origin and meaning of these figures, and of classical architectural details in general, remains obscure. It may be, for example, that the volute capitals of 'Ionic' columns, like those supporting the other two porticos of the Erechtheion, are stylized representations of the horns of sacrificed rams hung up on the building like trophies. Perhaps other ornamental features, like swags and festoons, egg and tongue mouldings, acanthus leaves and acroteria, have similar ritual origins. We don't know for sure. They remain mysterious, which makes their survival in the modern world all the more remarkable.

But to return to the caryatids, whatever their origins it seems perfectly clear that in the minds of the designers of the Erechtheion there was a connection between the idea of a column and the idea of a standing human figure. Could it be that all classical columns in some sense represent standing human figures? For centuries, architects and theorists have assumed this to be the case. A refinement of the theory is that Doric columns, like those on the Parthenon, represent sturdy male figures; Ionic columns, like those on the Erechtheion, represent matronly female figures; and Corinthian columns – a relatively late Greek invention – represent slender young girls. Well, in archaeological terms, this is very questionable, but that doesn't necessarily negate the general theory which seems in some primitive way to correspond to our inner

The Erechtheion stands opposite the Parthenon on the Acropolis. It is an asymmetrical composition of symmetrical elements. Here the 'order' is Ionic. Column capitals take the form of volutes or scrolls. But what do they represent? We do not know for sure, but their origin may lie in the horns of sacrificed rams, hung on the building like trophies.

The caryatids of the Erechtheion are clearly both structural columns and representations of people. Is there a sense in which otherwise abstract structural columns can be said to represent standing figures?

experience. Projecting human characteristics onto inanimate objects is something we do all the time, consciously or unconsciously. We see giants in the clouds, grasping hands in the branches of trees, faces in the fronts of houses – and standing figures in classical columns. The function of a column is to bear load, and we seem to feel the weight of that load, empathizing with the column as if it were a character in a drama. The caryatids are an artistic expression of a psychological truth. So classical columns represent human figures. This is a kind of representation we have not encountered so far. It is neither pictorial, like the Panathenaic frieze, nor reproductive, like the classical tradition, but symbolic, in a subtle and rather profound way. The broader idea now is that buildings can represent aspects of human experience. Standing upright and carrying a load may not seem a particularly important experience, but in its commonplace nature lies its strength. It is something the whole of humanity understands and shares.

Sometimes it is necessary to study the commonplace and restate the obvious in order to understand the most basic truths. For a figure to stand upright, there must be something to stand on – a ground; *the* ground – the surface of a planet exerting a gravitational pull on the figure itself and on the load it carries. There is a limit to the load that can be carried, a limit set by the characteristics of the human body and of the planet that it inhabits. If there is a ground, there must also be a sky, and between them a dividing line, the horizon. Body and planet are in perfect harmony. How could they be otherwise? The body evolved on the planet, adjusting itself over millions of years to these particular conditions. The planet in a sense gave birth to the body. They are inseparable. We experience the presence of ground and sky not just when we look out over a landscape but in every moment of our lives. The experience is so fundamentally human that we take it for granted and never talk about it. But perhaps we should. Perhaps we are missing the truth that lurks in the blindingly obvious. Now that we can fly in the air and travel to the moon, more than ever we need to remind ourselves that ground and sky are not just phenomena that we observe from an objective, scientific standpoint, but are a part of our very nature, locked into the form and substance of our bodies. It was ground and sky, horizon and gravity, horizontal and vertical that made us what we are, that made us able to stand upright and bear a load. So when we say that a classical column – or any column – represents a standing human figure, we are not saying anything trivial. We have hit upon something fundamental in the nature of architecture.

Regularity in architecture

Are there perhaps other ways in which architecture is symbolic of what we cannot avoid calling 'the human condition'? Yes, there are. Regularity is a quality that we normally associate with architecture. When we use architecture as a metaphor, when, for example, we talk about the 'architecture' of a novel, we are talking about ordered structure, the hidden regularities that hold the novel together and make it a coherent work of art. Looking again at the Parthenon, we note that its columns are identical and regularly spaced, that its double-pitched roof is symmetrical, and that its corners are right angles. Actually, as any student of ancient Greek architecture knows, part of that last sentence is not strictly true. The designers of the Parthenon have made some subtle adjustments to what would otherwise be a strict mathematical regularity. They have, for example, pushed the corner columns in slightly. You don't notice it at first, but when you do you realize that it is actually quite a big adjustment. The fact that you didn't notice it is important. One theory about this adjustment is that it corrects an optical illusion. If the columns were all evenly spaced, so the theory goes, then the corner columns would look as if they had been pushed out slightly. In other words, the row of columns would look irregular. So these adjustments, though they introduce a mathematical irregularity, only serve to show how important *apparent* regularity was to the ancient Greek architects.

There are different kinds and degrees of architectural regularity. Symmetry is a kind of regularity. A circular, domed building might be considered more symmetrical than a building like the Parthenon, which displays 'bilateral' rather than 'axial' symmetry. Bilateral symmetry is by far the most common kind in architecture. Is it perhaps in some way representational? Human bodies are, outwardly at least, bilaterally symmetrical, and this symmetry is not just observed from the outside but experienced from the inside. It affects the way we see the world, encouraging us to divide it into binary opposites – left and right, black and white, good and bad, yin and yang, on the one hand this, on the other hand that. So although a Greek temple looks nothing like a

The Jewish Museum in Berlin, designed by Daniel Libeskind. The irregularities of this building – angled walls, sloping floors, randomly placed windows – might be saying many different things, but one of them is: 'I am unusual because I don't conform to the regularities you expect in a piece of architecture'.

human body, nevertheless it shares with it this fundamental quality. It might be said to represent, at some level of consciousness, this aspect of human experience. Architectural symmetry is not always simple and unified as it is in the Parthenon. The symmetry of the Erechtheion, for example, is fragmented and complex. The component parts of the building – the rostrum, the north portico and the main body of the temple – are individually symmetrical, but the whole composition is asymmetrical. Nevertheless, despite these variations and others like them, it is true to say that most buildings display some degree of regularity and symmetry. And this applies equally to non-classical and non-western architectural traditions – to Gothic cathedrals, Mayan pyramids and Chinese palaces as much as to Greek temples. It even applies to the Modernist architecture of the last 100 years, despite the fact that certain factions in that movement were dedicated to the overthrow of 'outdated' concepts like regularity in general and symmetry in particular. Regularity is, as it were, architecture's default setting. When architects design irregular and radically asymmetrical buildings – the Deconstructivist buildings of the 1990s for example, like Daniel Libeskind's Jewish Museum in Berlin or Frank Gehry's Guggenheim in Bilbao – those buildings only really make sense as deliberate denials of the expected norm. That is their architectural meaning.

But what is the meaning of regularity? Why shouldn't buildings be irregular? Why shouldn't slanting columns, sloping floors and rhomboidal plans be the norm? The answer to this question is usually expressed in 'common sense' functional terms: it's not what people are used to, it's hard to fit the furniture in, the space is less usable, and so on. Like so much common sense, these assumptions are based more on prejudice than rational analysis. Possible constructional reasons for regularity are more persuasive. One might argue, for example, that it is cheaper and quicker to make all the columns and beams in a building the same size, which inevitably results in a regular, rectilinear layout. This is a very twentieth century explanation. In the age of mass production, we got used to the idea that repetition equals economy and efficiency. Henry Ford proved that If you want to make tens of thousands of cheap cars then you have to make them all the same. Presumably this principle applies equally to building components, especially if they are made in factories. In the middle of the twentieth century, certain architects got very worried by the possibility that the industrialization of building construction might result in an *excess* of regularity, that all buildings would begin to look the same and the environment would succumb to a dull visual monotony. Perhaps this happened to a degree in the high-rise housing estates of the 1960s and 1970s. But is architectural regularity always just the result of expediency in the construction process? Is that why all the columns of the Parthenon are the same? They certainly weren't mass produced in a factory. As far as we know, every stone was carved separately by hand on or near the site. It is possible that standardization of the columns and other repetitive components of the temple did make it easier to organize the building process. The historical record is sparse and we don't know for sure, but it may be that certain masons specialized in certain components – one might devote himself to column capitals, another to triglyphs – and this would improve the speed and efficiency of the whole process. But we should be wary of projecting the mental habits of the twentieth century (already becoming irrelevant, for different reasons, in the twenty-first) into the minds of architects and masons of the fifth century BC.

Visiting the Parthenon itself, as a ruin on the Acropolis or as displaced fragments in a museum, it becomes hard to believe that speed and efficiency were much in the minds of its creators. This is a monumental building, the house of a goddess and a symbol of the power of a great city. For Le Corbusier the Parthenon was 'one of the purest works of art that man ever made'.[3] The fact that it is a composition of repeated identical components seems to have more to do with its eternal symbolic meaning than with the efficiency of a construction process that lasted just few years. In the modern world, perfect standardization is easy to achieve with machines. Even a great work of art can be multiplied a million times and broadcast around the world for everyone to enjoy. We are still struggling to come to terms with the terrible implications of the power of mechanical, and now electronic, reproduction. According to the twentieth-century philosopher, Walter Benjamin, reproducing a work of art destroys its 'aura'.[4] It ceases to mean what it meant before. Perhaps it ceases to mean anything. But in a pre-industrial age, the carving by hand of 46 identical 10 metre (32.8 foot) high marble columns was almost a miracle. It was not easy; it was difficult and it was a sign of quality and worth. The regularity that modern architecture has inherited from ancient ancestors like the Parthenon has nothing to do with speed and efficiency. It is symbolic, not practical.

Rhythm in architecture

Regularity in architecture sometimes goes by another name: rhythm – a richer and more exciting word borrowed from music. Music is an art form that acts upon our minds and bodies more directly and immediately than painting or sculpture or architecture because it invites our participation: a band strikes up, a foot starts tapping, someone gets up to dance. There is an old cliché, usually attributed to the poet Goethe, that architecture is 'frozen music'. We think of buildings as three-dimensional objects, but architects and architectural theorists are always trying to inject the fourth dimension and set architecture in motion. A few buildings do literally move, but motion in architecture is more often imaginary. A row of equally spaced columns, like those on the side of the Parthenon, suggests a simple drum beat. The beat might be varied by altering the spacing, by changing the number of 'beats in a bar', or by superimposing more columns. The main portico of St Paul's Cathedral in London is supported by paired columns on two storeys, creating a rather complex rhythmic passage, like a fanfare or a drum roll. So regularity in architecture has a parallel in musical rhythm. It would

St Paul's Cathedral in London, designed by Sir Christopher Wren. Architecture is sometimes described in musical terms. The complex 'rhythm' of the columns at the entrance to St Paul's is like a trumpet fanfare.

be going too far to say that architecture deliberately 'represents' music, or even represents it subliminally in the way that a column represents a standing figure. It might be better to say that music and architecture hold rhythm in common, one creating it in sound over time, the other reflecting it in a static material composition.

But in both cases the rhythm is representational, and what it represents is an essential quality of human life. The drum beat and the row of columns are rhythmic because they were made by rhythmic beings, beings that breathe, with hearts that beat. If a single column represents a standing figure, a row of columns represents that figure in motion – walking and running, marching and dancing. Human motion is rhythmic in its nature. The regularity of the Parthenon is a pattern of rhythms within rhythms: the columns, the triglyphs, the grooves in the triglyphs, the little 'guttae' that hang from triglyphs like regular rain drops. Is it too fanciful to see in this hierarchical composition a representation not just of the rhythms of the human body, but of the rhythms of planet Earth, of days and months and years? These two rhythmic systems are, after all, intimately related. It is easier to think about architecture in these high flown terms when contemplating an ancient Greek temple' harder when looking at an ordinary house or factory or office block. But ordinary modern buildings have inherited their regularities and symmetries from their ancient ancestors and, at the deepest cultural level, they are equally symbolic and representational.

We have now identified several ways in which architecture can be said to be representational: a building can incorporate other representational arts like painting and sculpture; it can be, and often is, a representation of another building or of an earlier version of itself; by simple resemblance, buildings or parts of buildings can represent other important objects like human figures; common characteristics of architecture, like regularity and symmetry, can be seen as representations of aspects of human experience, like two handedness or the rhythm of breathing; and finally – an extension of the last – architecture can be seen as reflection of the primary conditions of a building's (and a human being's) existence on planet Earth.

The importance of meaning

But listing the different kinds of representation coldly like this seems to miss something essential in the concept. We started with a simple contrast between a building and a portrait, one abstract and functional, the other representational and functionless. Now, the concept of representation has turned out to be wider and deeper than we first thought. We can begin to see that it is not a limited activity associated with certain art forms but a general characteristic of human perception. We are representing things to ourselves and others all the time; it is the way we understand the world around us. Without representation, we could find no meaning in the world.

This ability to find meaning in the world is something so natural to us that we forget we have it. In waking hours, our minds and bodies are constantly interpreting our surroundings. The senses gather in, as it were, the raw data, and the mind converts that data into meaningful wholes. A certain configuration of shapes, colours, sounds and smells is compared with past experience and we decide, for example, that we are in a city street. This is not a passive process. We don't simply take in what's there, we interpret it – processing, comparing, composing – finding meaning in experience or, rather, actively projecting meaning onto experience.

One way to understand this ability to interpret is to imagine what life would be like without it. We can do this because, for a few unfortunate individuals, a meaningless world is a daily reality. *The Man Who Mistook His Wife for a Hat* is the title of one of many casebooks written for a lay readership by the clinical neurologist, Oliver Sacks. In the book, a certain Dr P visits Sacks's surgery complaining of a problem with his eyes. Sacks examines him thoroughly but can find nothing wrong until, observing him getting ready to leave, it becomes clear that he has difficulty recognizing everyday objects:

> 'He reached out his hand, and took hold of his wife's head, tried to lift it off, to put it on. He had apparently mistaken his wife for a hat!'[5]

In a later consultation, Sacks hands Dr P an item of clothing and asks him to describe it:

> 'A continuous surface,' he announced at last, 'infolded on itself. It appears to have... five outpouchings, if this is the word.'[6]

It was a perfect scientific description but clearly Dr P had completely failed to recognize a glove.

Dr P was an intelligent man and there was nothing wrong with his eyesight or any of his other senses, but his interpreting equipment had broken down and he could no longer find meaning in the world around him. What makes his case seem so strange is that it proves the existence of an ability we didn't realize we had in the first place.

By interpretation we build an inner world that philosophers call 'the intentional realm'. The intentional realm is not the real world but from the point of view of everyday experience it might as well be. Philosophers argue that since for most of us the intentional realm is indispensable and inescapable it is no less real than the 'real' world. When we physically alter our surroundings, by building a building perhaps, then a kind of negotiation takes place between the real world and the intentional realm. We can only build what is physically capable of being built, but we can also only build what we can imagine, what we can represent to ourselves and others.

The intentional realm is like an organising matrix, dividing the continuous, undifferentiated flow of sensory experience into manageable pieces, categorizing those pieces and composing them into meaningful wholes. When we see a continuous surface infolded on itself with five outpouchings we immediately think 'glove'. When we see a geometrically regular, delineated, transparent interruption in a continuous visual field of uniform colour and texture we immediately think, and 'see', a window. We are not born with this ability. It has to be learnt, like a language or at least a precondition for language. And language, it turns out, provides a useful analogy for thinking about architecture.

CHAPTER 2
LANGUAGE

In Chapter 1, architecture was seen not just as a practical craft but as a representational art and a conveyor of meaning. Looked at this way, it seemed able to tell simple but universal stories about what it's like to live the embodied, situated, rhythmic life of a human being on planet Earth. If architecture can convey meanings and tell stories, then is it perhaps some kind of language? On the face of it this is just a fanciful analogy. In most ways architecture is completely unlike language. Language is spoken and heard, or written and read. Either way it is a linear event unfolding over time, like music. Architecture, in contrast, is static and spatial, extended in three dimensions and able to be perceived, at least in some of its aspects, at one time. Nevertheless, the idea that architecture is a language, or at least resembles a language, is a common one in architectural theory. When the architectural historian, John Summerson, gave a series of radio talks in the 1950s about classical architecture, he called it 'The Classical Language of Architecture',[1] and when Charles Jencks wrote the book that inaugurated the style known as post-Modernism in the 1970s, he called it *The Language of Post-Modern Architecture.*[2]

There are some obvious ways in which architecture speaks to us. A building might, for example, tell us what it is, what function it performs. It might say 'I am a house' or 'I am a railway station'. This must happen, because people hardly ever mistake houses for railway stations. And it isn't just a matter of size. We don't mistake railway stations for apartment blocks either. We don't even mistake railway stations for heavy engineering factories, even though the spatial requirements of the two are rather similar. We seem to be able to 'read' buildings sufficiently well to make sense of them and find our way around the city, so they must in some way fulfil a similar function to spoken or written words. A linguist would say that they are signs or, more precisely, 'signifiers', and for every signifier there is at least one 'signified'. So the big building in the middle of town is a signifier and what it signifies is the building type for which the language signifier is the phrase 'railway station'.

Denotation and connotation

But it isn't quite as simple as that. In language, signifiers usually have more than one signified and often they have a whole hierarchy of signifieds of varying importance registered at different levels of a reader's consciousness. This is one of the ways in which poetry works. In a practical piece of writing, such as the directions for a journey, we do not expect the phrase 'railway station' to signify anything more than the building, pure and simple, but if we come across it in a poem we are likely to read a lot more into it. We know what the primary meaning is but we are alert for deeper layers of secondary meaning. These secondary meanings might be more abstract: 'travel', 'speed', 'luxury', 'punctuality'; and at another level: 'anxiety', 'romantic meetings', 'fond farewells', *'Brief Encounter'*. Sometimes the words 'denote' and 'connote' are used to distinguish between these different layers of meaning. The signifier denotes its primary meaning but it may also connote a whole array of secondary meanings, or 'connotations'.

If architecture is a language then perhaps it too makes use of denotation and connotation. The building might be a purely practical structure, the equivalent of the written directions for a journey, or it might be a built poem, rich in meaning. It is not hard to imagine how an actual built railway station might convey all those more abstract connotations listed above. St Pancras station in London, a Victorian building that was recently renovated and converted into a terminal for high speed trains to Paris and other European cities, illustrates this very well. The old roof of the train shed was retained by the architects for the restoration, even though it was too short for the new configuration of platforms and had to be extended. It might have been easier to have demolished it but that would have destroyed the atmosphere of the building. In other words, it would have changed its meaning by wiping out some of those romantic connotations. The designers wanted to emphasize those connotations, not destroy them, which is perhaps why they installed a big bronze statue of an embracing couple right under the crown of the arch, at the focal point of the space. There is not much subtlety about this piece of sculpture, which is a rather too obvious denotation of the idea 'romantic meeting'. More successful is the famous champagne bar nearby, said to be longest in the world, which takes the form of a single line of tables placed in line with the platforms as if it were an open train. It denotes its function plainly enough, but it also connotes some of those secondary meanings associated with rail travel, such as speed, luxury and romance. So abstract architecture in this case is communicating more poetically than figurative sculpture.

Notice that a speaker or writer, and by implication an architect, might or might not be aware of all the possible meanings that he or she has created. W. H. Barlow, the designer of the original St Pancras station (the train shed, not the Gothic revival hotel attached to its front, which was designed by George Gilbert Scott) was long dead in 1945 when the film *Brief Encounter* was made, yet for a certain section of the British

public, the romance of that film has become an inevitable connotation of every old railway station, including St Pancras. Language is a two way process involving readers (or listeners) and writers (or speakers) and the meaning that the reader receives is not necessarily what the writer intended. It might be better to say that writer and the reader both contribute to the meaning.

Sign systems

If architecture is like language it is because they are both sign systems. The study of sign systems, or rather the idea that almost every aspect of human culture can be studied as if it were a sign system, is called 'semiotics' and is closely related to the branch of linguistic philosophy called structuralism. In order to understand how sign systems work, we have to resort to some linguistic jargon, in particular the distinction between *parole* and *langue*. (The words are French because the concept was first formulated by the early twentieth-century Swiss linguist Ferdinand de Saussure.) *Parole* means individual utterances, spoken or written, like sentences. *Langue* refers to the whole body of the language that in some sense exists at any one time and from which the words that make up the individual utterances are chosen. We can visualize this as a diagram or chart, with the *parole* represented by the horizontal axis – imagine it being read from left to right over time like a written sentence – and *langue* represented by the vertical axis – imagine all the words that might have been chosen listed in columns beneath the words that were actually chosen. There are many versions of this idea and different linguists substitute different words for *parole* and *langue*. Some describe the axes of the diagram as 'diachronic' and 'synchronic', meaning extended over time and simultaneously available. Others

Buildings can be read. This building in Helsinki (left) was designed by Eliel Saarinen and completed in 1910. In its form and in the way it relates to its surroundings, it clearly conveys the message 'I am a railway station'. It might also convey more subtle messages about the importance of Helsinki as a modern city or about the romance of rail travel. Its style is sometimes described as 'national romantic'. The big statue in London's St Pancras station of a couple greeting one another (right) conveys the railway station message in a cruder, more literal way.

emphasize the distinction between the 'syntactic' nature of the horizontal axis, which is governed by the grammatical rules of the language, and the 'semantic', or meaning-generating, nature of the vertical axis. 'Message/code', 'historical/structural', 'conscious/unconscious', 'individual/collective', 'metonymical/metaphorical', 'syntagmatic/associative' and (one we have already encountered briefly) 'denotation/connotation': these are all different versions of the *parole/langue* idea. The distinction in music between melody and harmony is possibly another version, though the parallel is not exact.

It is very important to realize that the composing of a *parole* is not just a simple matter of choosing the right words for things, as if the relationship between words and things were fixed and static. The *parole/ langue* mechanism is more subtle than that. It doesn't just contain or organize meaning, it creates meaning. In most cases, the relationship between a word and a thing is completely arbitrary. Onomatopoeic words like 'buzz' or 'rumble', which actually sound like the sounds they stand for, are a possible exception, but ordinary words like 'house' or 'station' only mean what they mean because, over a very long period of time, English-speaking people have come to a tacit agreement on the matter. So the meaning of words is determined by tradition, not by any resemblance between word and thing. Meaning is also rather slippery and changeable. The same word can mean completely different things. For example, 'house' can mean 'dwelling', but it can also mean 'dynasty' or 'astrological sign' or a type of pop music. Meaning changes according context but context means more than just the sentence or *parole* a word finds itself in. Those long lists of possible words in the *langue* from which the single word was chosen are also a kind of context. It is the presence in the mind of the listener of other possible words that creates the meaning of the word actually heard. The meaning of a word is created by its *difference* from all the other words. To put it another way, meaning is not a positive but a negative thing. A word is defined by all the things it does *not* mean.

And, of course, on many occasions we deliberately use the 'wrong' word but still expect to be understood. In fact the listener's understanding can be richer and deeper when the wrong word is used. This is called 'metaphor'. When Lorenzo in *The Merchant of Venice* declares: 'How sweet the moonlight sleeps upon this bank!' he doesn't mean that the moonlight is actually sweet or actually asleep or could ever conceivably be either of those things in reality, and yet the meaning is perfectly clear.[3] And Shakespeare's choice of 'sweet' and 'sleeps' rather than, say, 'nicely' and 'shines', floods the sentence with multiple meanings. Partly it is surprise that creates such poetry. The less we expect a word or phrase, the more meaning it seems to carry. Tired old clichés like 'up with the lark' or 'no stone left unturned' started out as poetry but now fail to interest us much because they are what we expect to hear. On the other hand, a completely unexpected phrase that stretches its normal, agreed meaning almost to breaking point, can have a convulsive effect. It might, for example, make the listener burst out laughing.

Icon, index and symbol

How does all of this apply to architecture? One thing is clear: some of it doesn't really apply. We find it hard to accept, for example, that the relationship between signifier and signified in architecture could be entirely arbitrary, like the relationship between a word and the thing to which it refers. A flight of steps, for example, signifies the activity of ascending and descending on foot. It is hard to imagine it being used arbitrarily to signify some other activity like lying down to sleep or eating a meal with a group of friends. Of course both of these activities could take place on a flight of steps but there are other objects – beds and dining tables – that signify those activities more clearly. And they do so not because of tradition or convention but because there is something intrinsic to the form and feel of them that corresponds to or suggests the activities they signify. A person brought up always to sleep on the ground might not immediately be able to read the significance of a bed, but they could probably guess it before long. Not knowing the language would only be a temporary barrier to meaning.

We have to turn to the American philosopher, Charles Sanders Peirce, for a concept more obviously relevant to architecture.[4] Believing that human culture was essentially sign-based, Peirce tried to develop a complete classification system for signs, or rather for the different types of relationship between signifiers and signifieds. Three of his sign categories were: Icon, Index and Symbol. By Symbol he meant the kind of relationship that a word has to a thing – an arbitrary link, sanctioned only by tradition and not relying on any kind of resemblance. This, as we have seen, is only of limited interest to architectural theory. The other two seem more pertinent. An Icon is a signifier that resembles the thing it signifies, in the way that a painted portrait resembles the person portrayed. And an Index is a signifier that 'points to' the thing it signifies, like a road sign pointing to a destination.

Here we seem to be firmly in architectural territory. The architects of big, complex buildings like hospitals and airports are always worrying about the 'legibility' of their buildings, by which they mean the very practical question of whether or not people will be able to find their way around. 'Signage' becomes an important part of the design, and it is generally agreed that the less signage you need the better the building is from the point of view of legibility. This implies that a perfectly legible building would be able to do without signage altogether. Its circulation spaces – entrance halls, corridors, staircases, landings, lift lobbies – would indicate to the visitor which way they should go purely by means of form, scale and juxtaposition. In other words, the parts of the building would be acting as signifiers of the Index type, literally pointing people in the right direction.

The Index, then, is a type of signifier especially relevant to architecture. What about the Icon? This too is relevant, but in a subtler way. Architectural steps don't look anything like human feet but their treads and risers have the dimensions of human feet and match human physical capabilities. They therefore resemble or picture the activity of walking. In other words they signify it in an iconic way. Let's consider an actual flight of steps in a great work of architecture: Michelangelo's Laurentian Library in Florence. The entrance hall of the library is a rather

The vestibule of the Laurentian Library in Florence, designed by Michelangelo. The famous staircase signifies its function clearly enough but has myriad other connotations. It seems to tumble out of the door of the library like a waterfall in a cave. Perhaps the division into three parts – a main flight flanked by secondary flights – reflects the social hierarchy of its users.

confined, vertical space, richly ornamented by recessed columns and blank windows or aedicules. Its basic function is to accommodate the staircase that leads up to the entrance of the library proper. And what a staircase it is, perhaps the most famous in the whole history of western architecture. It signifies its function in a straightforward way like any other staircase, but it also signifies many other things, including all the monumental staircases that preceded it in the long history of western classical architecture, going right back to ancient Rome. It is as if Michelangelo were trying to sum up that history and simultaneously transcend it by realizing its full poetic potential for the first time.

The staircase works beautifully as a means to get from level A to level B but its artistic purpose is to dignify that function. One of the ways it does this is by dividing itself into three parts. Two massive balustrades, themselves monumental pieces of architecture, define a wide central flight of curved steps while seeming to exclude outer flights which are plain and straight. These outer flights have no balustrades of their own and rise only to the shared landing two thirds of the way up. What does it signify, this hierarchy of major and minor, curved and straight? Perhaps it corresponds to a social hierarchy. Imagine a member of the Medici family sweeping up the main flight while his attendants take the secondary routes, waiting patiently on either side of the landing before entering the library after him. So the form of the staircase signifies, iconically, the relative status of its users. Tourists often get no further than the vestibule – it has become a destination in its own right – but if they do proceed into the library they experience an extreme spatial contrast, a sudden switch from vertical to horizontal. A long straight, pilastered hall lies before them, with big windows on both sides casting their light onto ranks of desks. Perhaps it is the tension between the two spaces, library and vestibule, that creates the illusion that, in the other direction, the staircase itself is in motion, tumbling or flowing out of the bright library into the relative gloom of the vestibule. The iconic mode of signification has now

become truly poetic, recalling associations buried deep in the language, not just of architecture but of landscape and the natural world. We think of rocks, caves and waterfalls.

Ambiguity and double coding

So Peirce's concepts of Index and Icon seem to work better for architecture than the analogy with words. But the basic *parole/langue* mechanism remains the same and we can identify more ways in which it operates in architecture. For example, some architectural theorists have laid great emphasis on ambiguity and what they call 'double coding'. Of course, in spoken or written language, ambiguity is usually a bad thing, a breakdown of syntax leading only to confusion. But this is to ignore its poetic potential. In 1930, the literary critic William Empson explored this potential in a book called *Seven Types of Ambiguity* (his first type was Metaphor). The Empson of the architectural world is Robert Venturi whose book, *Complexity and Contradiction in Architecture,* was published in 1966. Venturi's message was basically that a building can, like a poem, mean several things at the same time. To see how this works we can do no better than examine briefly one of Venturi's own buildings, the house that he built in Philadelphia for his mother, Vanna Venturi, at about the same time that he wrote the book.

It is a small house, with only five habitable rooms, but it looks big because it puts up a unified front in the form of a shallow-pitched gable like a classical pediment. Already it is clear that a language is being used, a language that most people understand. At the simplest level, this form clearly signifies 'house'. It has been chosen from many possible profiles for this reason. But its meaning is more precise than

that. It might even signify a particular house from the canon of architectural history, and in fact we know that it was influenced by McKim Mead & White's 'shingle-style' Low House built in 1887. The references don't stop there though, for this is a broken pediment and its precedents go further back, to Michelangelo and Vanbrugh, whose Mannerist and Baroque architecture Venturi admired on study trips to Europe. The main entrance to the house is in the middle, so the facade is basically symmetrical, like a child's drawing of house. And yet at the same time it is asymmetrical, because there are two square windows (bedroom and bathroom) on the left and one long horizontal window (kitchen) on the right. These are very ordinary windows, with thin frames almost flush with the stucco wall, yet they too carry their share of meaning. The long kitchen window seems to have been borrowed from a different language of architecture – the early Modernism of Le Corbusier, perhaps. So is this a traditional or a modern house? Of course, it is both.

We have not yet got past the front entrance, and already the ambiguities are piling up. Inside, the plan of the house is simple in outline but complex in its space divisions, with angled walls, curved ceilings, recessed windows and rooms that might be inside or might be outside. The living room has a traditional focal point in the form of a hearth that is generous but still too small to justify the big chimney that we might have noticed outside, behind the break in the pediment. What is even stranger about this hearth, however, is that it seems to be fighting for space with the staircase, which has to shrink to squeeze past it. All this ambiguity and inconsistency, complexity and contradiction, is, of course, deliberate.

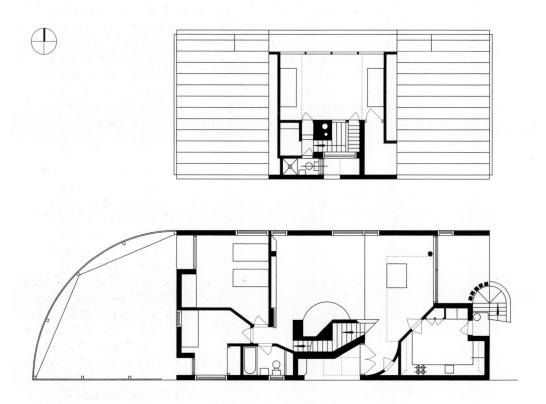

Ambiguity can be poetic, or funny, or just confusing, but it can also be useful. It might even help solve modern architecture's biggest problem: its unpopularity. Modern architecture is perhaps no more unpopular than modern painting or modern music or modern poetry, but its unpopularity matters more because it is a public art and is often paid for by the public. One possible solution to this problem is to give the public what it wants, which usually means something traditional, something in a language that ordinary people understand. Architects find this very difficult because for the past 60 years or so their education has led them to value innovation more than tradition. They think they can improve on tradition, and they think that they know best.

Robert Venturi and his wife, Denise Scott Brown, thought about this problem a lot, and in their 1972 book, *Learning from Las Vegas,* they suggested some possible solutions. They thought Modernist architecture was dull and boring, insignificant (literally) and uncommunicative, overvaluing simplicity and consistency when the world around was becoming ever more complex and contradictory. They wanted their architecture to embrace the ambiguities of modern life by being popular and elitist at the same time. So it would have to speak to ordinary people in a language they could relate to, and at the same time speak to sophisticated people, like architectural colleagues and competitors, in a more elevated language. It would have to be 'double coded'. We can see how this works in the Vanna Venturi house. Anybody can see that it's a house. The pitched-roof profile, the apparently solid walls perforated

Ground and upper-level plans of the Vanna Venturi House. Notice how the staircase seems to have to fight for its space with the fireplace. Although the basic footprint of the plan is a simple rectangle, the rooms are all different and characterized by unique spatial events such as curved and angled walls. All have their meanings.

by ordinary windows, the chimney – all come from the language of
traditional domestic architecture. The average passer-by, seeing only
these unremarkable features, registers vague approval but otherwise
remains uninterested. An architect, however, immediately detects
something strange, a sort of wrongness, but a knowing not a naïve
wrongness, and begins to read the house at a deeper level, as
one might read a poem. Before long they will be spotting broken
pediments, Corbusian windows and references to the shingle style.

Aesthetic intentions

There is a more general point here about aesthetic intentions in both
language and architecture. We have seen how, in spoken language, an
unexpected word or phrase seems to carry extra meaning, to pack a
bigger punch than an everyday phrase or a cliché. This is surely also
true of architecture. Venturi's sophisticated ordinariness works by
distorting conventional elements and combining them in unexpected
ways; by using far-fetched words and messing about with normal
syntax. An ordinary, non-architectural house builder will use reasonably
proportioned windows and put them in the expected places. But take
just one of those windows and make it slightly larger, perhaps put it up
against the side wall of the room rather than in the middle (this applies
to all of the windows in the Vanna Venturi house) and immediately a
knowing observer will get the message that this is a work with aesthetic
intentions. It is competing in a different field and speaking a different
language or rather, in Venturi's case, speaking a heightened, poetic
version of the same language.

Messing about with the syntax is easier to spot when the
grammatical rules of the language are well established, as they are
in western classical architecture. The sixteenth-century Mannerist
architect, Giulio Romano, delighted in architectural solecisms such as
unevenly spaced pilasters, off-centre windows, fractured entablatures
and string courses that became pediments. At this distance it's hard to
say exactly what these irregularities meant. Historians usually resort
to vague adjectives like 'playful' or 'unsettling'. In modern architecture
the grammatical rules are less strict and operate in a more general
way but we still expect, for example, the heavier parts of a building to
be at the bottom and lighter parts at the top. And if that expectation is
overturned, then we look for the structure – a row of columns, perhaps –
that makes this possible.

Rem Koolhaas is perhaps a Mannerist, because he enjoys thwarting
expectations. The house that he designed for a wheelchair-bound client
in Bordeaux takes expectation-thwarting as its guiding principle. The
first thing you notice is an enormous block of rough concrete, itself the
size of a house, apparently hovering unsupported over an open terrace.
Part of the terrace is enclosed by big sheets of glass, but where are the
columns? It's a kind of conjuring trick. In fact there are no conventional
columns anywhere in this large, three storey building (the lowest level is
dug into the hillside). What does this mean? To banish the column, the
very symbol of architecture itself, is surely a kind of rebellion, a rejection
of all grammatical rules? The same principle is applied to all the other
elements of the building: staircases, doors, windows, balustrades – all are

Two Mannerist buildings: the Palazzo del Te (above) designed by Giulio Romano in the 1520s, and the Bordeaux House designed by Rem Koolhaas in the 1990s (left). In their very different ways, both break architectural conventions in order to excite the onlooker. In the palazzo, classical details are misused like deliberate grammatical errors; in the house, a massive concrete block seems to hover in the air.

reinvented and made almost unrecognizable, refusing to signify their function in the normal way. The most useful of these reinventions is the lift which takes the form of an open room, furnished as a study.

In linguistic terms, Koolhaas's refusal to allow things to speak plainly for themselves might be described as irony. Irony, like its more abrasive cousin, sarcasm, is just saying the opposite of what you mean ('Oh, brilliant!') and this, surely is what Koolhaas's Bordeaux house does. A concrete block hovering in the air says: 'Look, I'm solid and earthbound (not)'. But the irony is rather heavy and paradoxically the effect is only to confirm the sovereignty of language. If the language didn't exist, there would be no need to rebel against it. (The big concrete block, which contains the bedrooms, is actually supported at one end by a discreet portal frame and at the other by a concrete cylinder trying desperately to disguise itself in a sleeve of reflective stainless steel to avoid being recognized as a column.)

Once you get the idea that architecture is a language, it's hard to let go of it. Yet that is precisely what the Modernist architects of the early twentieth century tried to do. They were interested in function, not meaning. They believed that a building could be like a piece of engineering – a purely practical solution to a functional problem – and that beauty would follow naturally from utility. Venturi's revival of ambiguity, and the language-based post-Modernist architecture that followed it in the 1970s and 1980s, was a reaction against a prevailing Modernist orthodoxy. Modernism, or at least the functionalist wing of the movement, was so keen to suppress traditional language that it even coined new words to describe buildings and parts of buildings. Houses became dwelling units, windows became fenestration, walls became cladding, streets became circulation routes. The analogy was with science, not language. What the Modernists forgot, of course, was that language is always present, whether you welcome it or not.

Perhaps, in the end, the real force of the language model in architecture lies not in linguistic technicalities like *parole* and *langue*, index and icon, but in the simple realization that architectural meaning is inevitably something shared and traditional. It is possible to conceive of a private language, such as might be used by lovers, but mostly languages are shared by large groups of people. (A language used by only one person – a code for diary entries, perhaps – is the opposite of a language because it is a form of *non*-communication.) The people that share a language also create that language. Every time anybody writes or speaks a sentence, the language is altered very slightly. That sentence will make an infinitesimally small contribution to the slow drift of meaning as words shift in relation to each other like grains of sand on a beach. But it isn't just the writers and speakers that are active in the development of language; listeners and readers are equally important. A sentence written a hundred years ago does not mean now what it meant then. The dictionary definitions of the words might be the same, but their connotations will have shifted. The context, including everything that has been spoken or written since, is different, so the meaning is different. We are reading the sentence, as it were, with the benefit of hindsight.

Creating architectural meaning

This shared nature of language has profound implications for architecture and architects. It means that the 'readers' of architecture – clients, building users, passers-by – are co-responsible with the architects for the creation of architectural meaning. A building means not what the architect intends it to mean but what all of the users of the language of architecture will allow it to mean. There is nothing mysterious about this; we encounter it all the time in ordinary conversations about architecture. In the 1960s and 1970s, when mass housing was being designed in a tired and debased Modernist style, people were always comparing the high rise towers and slab blocks with prisons. One south London housing estate was known locally as Alcatraz. The architect may well have

This portal of the fifteenth-century monastery of Champmol in Dijon is famous for its sculpture (Philip the Bold and his wife introduced to the Virgin, by Claus Sluter) but its architectural frame is what interests us here. The pointed Gothic arch was a solution to a structural problem but it has become an almost universally recognized symbol of piety.

protested that his design didn't 'really' mean that. But no single person can decide such a thing because language is shared, and meaning must always be negotiated.

It is perhaps theoretically possible to devise a new language, but it will be a poor thing in comparison with the language that we learnt in the years before we even knew that we were learning. Language is traditional, something handed down, not invented, and this applies also to the language of architecture. Architectural forms only become meaningful with the passage of time. Take the pointed arch, for example. For most westerners just a glimpse of this simple form, however crudely represented, immediately signifies a cluster of ideas connected with religion: church, Christianity, piety, prayer. When Victorian architects built churches they chose the Gothic or 'pointed' style because it had the right connotations. They didn't decide on the meaning; the meaning had already been decided by tradition. It is not surprising, then, that post-Modernist architects, having readopted the language model, often revived historical forms. Ordinary city office blocks that in the 1960s would have been plain glass boxes, in the 1980s were dressed up like Roman temples. The fashion didn't last long, perhaps because by then the supposedly 'dumb' Modernist box had itself entered the language and come to mean 'office block', but it was a kind of desperate bid to communicate, to give architecture a voice once again.

Now, post-Modernism is itself a historical style, and is widely reviled among progressive architects. As a result, the language model has largely fallen into disuse as a way of thinking about architecture. Modernism has reasserted itself in a new guise. The idea that the main purpose of architecture is not to communicate but to invent new forms, often now with the help of computers, has gained currency once again. For some architects, the stranger the form, the better. Novelty has supplanted intelligibility. Those two fundamental characteristics of language – its shared and traditional nature – are antithetical to an architectural culture that values only novelty, invention and individual creativity. But language never goes away. Buildings will always have meaning, and architects who refuse to recognize this are deceiving themselves.

Deconstruction

We can't leave the subject of language and architecture without saying something about Deconstruction. The word has obvious architectural connotations, though as a mode of philosophical enquiry it originally had nothing to do with architecture. It was coined by the French philosopher Jacques Derrida. Derrida was what is now known as a post-Structuralist, that is to say he continued the semiotic and structuralist tradition founded by Saussure but disagreed with certain important aspects of it. His main objection to the Saussure's signifier/signified model of language was its implication that of these two terms, the second was more important. The objection seems unreasonable at first. Language refers to, is 'about', things in the world. Those things must surely exist before language can deal with them? The signified must therefore be 'prior to' the signifier. Not so, according to Derrida. His argument begins by questioning the priority that Saussure and other linguists give to speech over writing. Again common sense would seem to be on Saussure's side. Surely all languages first existed as speech and only later were written down. But by a careful analytical study – a 'deconstruction' – of various philosophical texts, by the eighteenth-century philosopher Jean-Jacques Rousseau, for example, and by Saussure himself, Derrida detects certain inconsistencies in the use of metaphor that betray a fundamental paradox in the relationship between speech and writing.[5] What the texts intend to say is that speech comes before writing, but the implication of what they actually say is that writing comes before speech. In general terms, the idea is that every spoken utterance, every *parole*, no matter how urgent or immediate it might be – a cry for help, perhaps – depends on an arbitrary, abstract system of differences that exists independently of the person making the utterance. Writing is such a system. Writing depends neither on the presence of the person that creates it nor on the presence of what it refers to. The meaning of a text is always provisional and approximate. And since human beings can only understand their world by means of language and other sign systems, which are kinds of texts, they can never attain complete knowledge of anything in that world. Signs signify other signs, which in turn signify other signs in an endless chain. There can be no fixed, permanent, 'transcendent' reality to which language refers. Meaning is endlessly 'deferred', never completely decided. The project of philosophy as conceived in western culture is therefore impossible. Deconstruction sees itself not as another philosophical system, like Platonism or logical positivism, but as an activity or process by which we remind ourselves of the limits of language and thought.

When Deconstruction is applied to the sign system called architecture, the argument becomes even more convoluted. Architecture and philosophy are, it turns out, related in rather fundamental ways. Think how often architecture provides metaphors for thought itself. We talk about the 'structure' of a philosophical system, about opinions that are 'well founded', about the 'embellishment' of an argument. It is as if

The circulation spine of the Wexner Center at Ohio State University (1983–89) by Peter Eisenman is defined not by functional walls and roofs but by a purely symbolic framework, as if it were in the process of being constructed – or deconstructed.

architecture were itself a kind of philosophy – a set of ideas about the fixed, logical, stable relationships between things. It is the architectural aspect of philosophy that Derrida objects to most – the idea that it is possible to take an overview of reality, to see how one part relates to another and thereby to understand it. Even that word 'understand' has faint architectural resonances. Deconstruction dismisses all such notions as mere comforting illusions. It sounds like something architects should steer well clear of but in the 1980s certain architects, notably Peter Eisenman and Bernard Tschumi, adopted Deconstruction as the basis (if one can use such a word in this context) of a new kind of architecture. They even went so far as to involve Derrida himself in their enterprise. The result was a curious, hybrid style that came to be know as Deconstructivism. The word combines Deconstruction with Constructivism, the name given to experimental Russian architecture of the years immediately following the 1917 revolution.

Collision and combination

Deconstructivism first came to the public's attention in an exhibition called Deconstructivist Architecture held at the Museum of Modern Art in New York in 1988, which included projects by Eisenman and Tschumi, with others by Frank Gehry, Zaha Hadid, Coop Himmelb(l)au, Rem Koolhaas and Daniel Libeskind.[6] These architects did not all share an enthusiasm for, or even a knowledge of, the philosophy of Jacques Derrida, but they did share a desire to destroy the general formal coherence of conventional architecture, whether traditional or Modernist. Their buildings – mostly at this stage just projects – were assemblages of fragments, distorted and juxtaposed in apparently random combinations. The point was not to devise a coherent system into which elements like walls and roofs, columns

Plan of the Wexner Center. The campus grid and the city grid collide, destroying the rectilinear consistency that one might normally expect of such a plan. Overlapping grids of this kind were to become a cliché of would-be Deconstructivist architecture for the next ten years.

and beams, and windows and doors could fit, but to do the opposite: to let those elements collide and combine in unpredictable ways.

One of the earliest built Deconstructivist buildings was the Wexner Center for the Arts at Ohio State University in Columbus, designed by Peter Eisenman and completed in 1989. An important feature of this building is the way it aligns itself with both the street grid of Columbus and the planning grid of the existing university campus. The two grids happen to lie at an angle of 12.25 degrees to one another. This dual alignment destroys the rectilinear consistency that one might normally expect, putting the various elements of the plan, such as main circulation spine and the galleries and auditoriums that it serves, into a deliberately awkward juxtaposition. The trick of overlaying angled grids was to become something of a cliché in would-be Deconstructivist designs for the next ten years or so. But the Wexner has other unexpected features. That circulation spine, for example, is marked not by a functional enclosure but by a purely symbolic open framework or scaffolding which seems to imply that it is in the process of being constructed, or deconstructed. And at one end of the spine stands a somewhat literal recreation of the castle-like college armoury that used to stand on the site, except that its turrets and arches have been sliced through in a seemingly arbitrary manner as if to deny any straightforward reference to the old building, or in other words any simple equivalence of signifier and signified.

Another, smaller Eisenman project of the same period, the Koizumi Sangyo Corporation building in Tokyo, is like the deconstruction of a philosophical text re-enacted in architectural terms. The existing text is a straightforward, curtain-walled office building designed by another architect. Eisenman's interventions take the form of two roughly cubic volumes inserted into, or perhaps growing out of, opposite corners of the building. These volumes are composed of L-shaped elements at different scales and set at different angles so that they disrupt both the space itself and the user's, or reader's, perception of it. The result has a pleasing complexity, like a three dimensional Cubist painting.

For Eisenman, there was a conscious connection between these projects and the philosophy of Deconstruction. But it would be wrong to see Deconstruction as prior to Deconstructivism. It was not the philosophical basis of the style. Frank Gehry had been experimenting with disruptive geometries since the 1970s and Zaha Hadid's astonishing Hong Kong Peak project of 1982 predated the period when the name Derrida was on every intellectually inclined architect's lips. At the time, Hadid was described by the critic and historian Kenneth Frampton as a 'Kufic Suprematist', referring to her Arabic origins and the influence of Kasimir Malevich's early twentieth-century Suprematist paintings on her work. Deconstruction and Deconstructivism were perhaps parallel or equivalent movements, but they were not directly related to one another as theory is to practice.

One of Zaha Hadid's exuberant paintings of her 1982 competition-winning project for a club on the Peak in Hong Kong (opposite). The club is the dark angled form right at the top of the painting. Is this Deconstructivist? Perhaps, but it preceded the period when Jacques Derrida became a fashionable reference point for advanced architectural theorists.

The Koizumi Sangyo Corporation building in Tokyo (left). Peter Eisenman's alterations to an existing building are like the deconstruction of a philosophical text reenacted in architectural terms.

CHAPTER 3
FORM

Form and matter – the shape of a thing and the material that it's made of – are inseparable companions. Everything that physically exists has both form and matter. Even a 'formless' mass has some kind of form, like a cloud or a heap, and form devoid of matter is a mere ghost or apparition. So why do we, in language and thought, persistently treat form and matter as if it were possible to separate them? This is a question that has troubled philosophers for thousands of years. For Plato, the distinction between form and matter was connected with thinking itself. One place that form might exist without matter is in the human mind. When we think of a cat or a tree, we 'form' these objects in our mind and perhaps we even see them with the mind's eye even though they contain no matter. Plato elevated form to the status of the divine by thinking of it as existing in the mind of God (or of the demiurge that he imagined as the creator of the world). Form, for Plato, was therefore more important than matter because it was eternal and unchanging. The form of a cat will always exist, he thought, whereas the matter of which a particular cat is made will soon be disappearing into the earth and taking some other form. So his idea was that each individual, materially constituted cat was really just a passing reflection on Earth of an ideal, celestial, eternal cat existing in the mind of God.[1]

Aristotle didn't think it necessary to postulate ideal forms. For him, it was enough to observe that form obviously in some sense existed in the real world, even if it was inseparable from matter. Aristotle's version of form was not eternal and unchanging but constantly in motion, like matter. He argued that the form that comes to mind when we think of a cat only represents that cat at one stage in its life. It has also been an embryo in its mother's womb and it will eventually be a pile of bones. Aristotle saw both form and matter as dynamic. They were two of the driving forces behind a changing but purposeful world. He included them in what has become known as his 'doctrine of the four causes', the other

The Naiku Shrine at Ise in Japan. The building has been rebuilt every 20 years since the seventh century. So how old is it? Twelve years or 1,200 years? It depends whether we are talking about its form or the matter in which that form is realized. The relationship between form and matter is an important theme in architectural theory.

two types of cause being the 'efficient' cause, which means the active agent that makes something happen (this is the type of cause to which we most often apply our modern word 'cause'), and the 'final' cause, which means the underlying purpose of an object or an event. So, for example, in the formal cause of a house would be the architect's design, the material cause would be the bricks and mortar, the efficient cause would be the builder and the final cause would be the function of the house as a place to live in. But the important thing from our point of view is that Aristotle not only accepted the unreal distinction between form and matter, he reinforced it by making it an essential part of his model of the world.[2]

Modern concepts like Darwinian evolution have superseded Plato's and Aristotle's ideas about the way the world works, but even Darwin couldn't help talking about form and matter as if they were separable. It is an idea lodged unshakeably in our language and thought. And it is an idea central to architectural theory. As designers of objects to be made, architects deal fundamentally with the relationship between form and matter. The Naiku Shrine at Ise in Japan provides a striking illustration of this relationship. The shrine is important for lots of reasons. It is the Shinto Religion's most sacred site and it is built in an architectural style known as Shinmeizukuri, which is reserved specially for it. But it is the regular ritual renewal of the shrine that illuminates the question of form and matter. Every 20 years, the building is dismantled and reassembled on an adjacent site. It oscillates, as it were, between its two sites on a twenty year frequency. This has so far happened 61 times since the building of the first shrine in the seventh century. So how many buildings are there? One, or two, or 62? Where is the real building? On site A or site B? And how old is it really? Twelve years or 1,200 years? The only way to answer these questions sensibly is to separate form from matter. The form, with its raised floor, encircling veranda and simple double-pitched roof, is ancient; the matter – wood and thatch – is new.

There is a cultural difference here between Japanese and western attitudes to the preservation of important buildings. In nineteenth-century England, the Society for the Protection of Ancient Buildings fought against the wholesale restoration of medieval churches in which original ornament was replaced by modern imitations. The members of SPAB valued the old stones themselves. Matter was as important to them as form. But in Japan, as we have seen, matter is relatively unimportant. Its transience is accepted, whereas form is preserved at all costs.

The separation of form and matter

One way that architects separate form from matter is in their drawings. Drawing and designing are closely related activities. The design in the mind is drawn on the paper, and what is drawn is the form of the object without the matter that will eventually constitute it. Of course, objects that already exist can be drawn, and in this case the form is abstracted from the material object. But the essence of architecture, as we commonly think of it, lies in the activity of designing and drawing, of imagining form and representing it in a convenient medium. This automatically gives precedence to form over matter. But need this necessarily be so? Is it possible to create a building without design? One can easily imagine how a simple building – a primitive shelter, perhaps – might be roughly assembled from readily available materials without the help of a drawing. But it's very hard to imagine a man-made building being created purely spontaneously, without any design, however rudimentary and provisional, being present in the mind of the builder. The act of building inevitably involves design of some kind, which in turn involves the separation of form from matter.

De re aedificatoria, by Leon Battista Alberti, is the earliest and most important architectural treatise of the Renaissance. It was written in the 1450s and, like the ancient work by Vitruvius on which it was loosely modelled, it is divided into ten books. In the standard English translation, the titles of the first two books are: 'Lineaments' and 'Materials'. In other words form and matter. For Alberti, form was the architect's first concern, and the only respectable architectural forms for important public buildings such as churches, or 'temples' as he called them, were those borrowed from ancient Rome and revived after more than a thousand years of Gothic barbarity. Materials were important too, of course, but whether a building was built in stone or brick or wood, it still had to 'conform' to ancient Roman precedent. So the relationship between form and matter was rather loose.

This is characteristic of most Renaissance architecture. In Gothic architecture form and matter are much more closely related. We might even go so far as to say that Gothic architectural form was, to some extent, determined by the nature of the building materials used. The pointed arch and the ribbed vault can be seen as the ultimate expression of the structural potential of un-reinforced stone construction. We will return to this question of the relationship between architectural form and building materials in Chapter 5. We can never completely ignore it. Nevertheless, for the remainder of this chapter, we will, like Alberti, concentrate mainly on pure form or 'lineaments'.

Drawings and design

It is worth exploring the question of drawing in more detail in order to prepare the ground for the main subject of this chapter: proportion. Not all drawings are line drawings. Shapes can be depicted by areas of colour (including black and white) which represent light and shade, and the textures and colours of the materials in the real object. A pure line drawing is a more abstract construction because it ignores the visible effects of light. The lines in a line drawing are an artificial device to represent the profiles, junctions, edges, boundaries and horizons of surfaces. They delineate form, not matter, and they are not visible in the real object. One might argue that some objects, such as buildings, do display visible lines – the mortar joints in brickwork, for example, or the glazing bars of a curtain wall. But these are really long narrow surfaces, quite different from the notional, symbolic lines of a drawing.

There are many different types of architectural drawing but the most fundamental distinction is between a drawing of something that already exists and a drawing of something proposed: a design. Architects are traditionally expected to have some skill in both of these types of drawing and in practice it is sometimes hard to distinguish between them. An architect's perspective drawing of a proposed building in its existing setting might fool an innocent observer into thinking that the building already exists. The digital pasting of perspective drawings into photographs now routinely fools even the not-so-innocent observer. But this distinction between the existing and the proposed is important for another reason. It highlights the question of what counts as architecture and what does not. We could be very strict and say that the word architecture should only be applied to real buildings; not until the design has actually been realized on the site does it attain the status of architecture. But this would exclude lots of perfectly buildable designs that, through no fault of their own, failed to get built. Surely such designs should be allowed into the architectural territory where they can make their contribution to the progress of the craft? Architectural history is full of them – Adolf Loos's 1922 competition-losing design for the Chicago Tribune building, for example, or Zaha Hadid's 1982 competition-winning design of the Peak in Hong Kong (see page 41). At one more remove from reality are those designs which no one, not even their authors, ever seriously thought would be built. Visionary urban projects like Le Corbusier's Ville Radieuse or Frank Lloyd Wright's Broadacre City might come into this category. Unrealistic they may have been, from a social and economic point of view, but nobody would exclude them from the category 'architecture' if only because of the enormous influence they have had on the development of real cities.

Even if visionary urban projects like Frank Lloyd Wright's Broadacre City are only ever realized in imperfect and fragmentary forms, it doesn't mean that they don't count as 'architecture'. Buildings are architecture, but projects are architecture too, and some of them have been more influential than buildings.

Could Stephen Perrella and Rebecca Carpenter's Möbius House exist outside a computer? Probably not. Although there are suggestions of real materials and even, in the thin curved bars, what looks like a structure to resist gravity, it would surely look very different if actually built. Here we are perhaps at the limit of what can reasonably be called architecture.

But what about the pure fantasies – those designs that are not just unlikely to be built but are actually unbuildable because they fail to take account of the primary conditions for the existence on Earth of large objects like buildings? Perhaps they postulate some magic material that doesn't really exist, or depend on the suspension of an inescapable natural force like gravity. Is this where we should set the boundary of architecture's territory? When does a design become a mere doodle? It is hard to imagine a project like Stephen Perrella and Rebecca Carpenter's Möbius House existing anywhere but in the virtual reality of the computer, yet Perrella and Carpenter are certainly architects and perhaps their unbuildable projects are architecture of a kind. One might even argue that architecture, as an art or craft, is better represented by drawings and designs than it is by real buildings. A drawing can be a representation of an existing building, in which case the building takes priority. But in architecture the situation is reversed. The drawing takes priority and the building, when it is built, is a representation of the drawing.

When we delineate a building that does not yet exist – when we make a design, in other words – we are trying to get some idea of what it will look like. Or are we? It depends what type of drawing we choose. If we draw an illusionistic perspective then we are certainly trying to do that. But what if we want to work out how the walls are going to be connected to the roof? We might decide that a section drawing would be more useful for this purpose, and the section might show parts that are not going to be visible in the finished building. And it would probably be important, in working out this detail, to see the sizes of the various components – brick walls and wooden rafters, say – in accurate

relation to each other. In other words we should draw the building 'to scale'. So there are two main types of design drawing: those that give an impression of what the building will look like, typified by the perspective, and those that are drawn accurately to scale, typified by so called 'orthographic' drawings like plans, sections and elevations. Orthographic drawings do not represent things as they are seen; they represent things as they are, or will be. An elevation of the facade of a building, drawn accurately to scale, presents an image which is impossible to find in the real world without some artificial aid, like a camera with a perspective correcting lens. Our eyes see things, roughly speaking, in perspective, not in elevation, and there is no way to alter this fact. This is not just a technical or procedural matter; it has profound theoretical implications, as we shall see.

To recap briefly: architects imagine buildings in their minds and represent these mental images in drawings of one kind or another, including those made with computers. By their very nature, these drawings deal mainly with form and only secondarily with matter, or materials. It is perfectly possible to draw a form without knowing what it will be made of, but it is completely impossible to draw formless matter. Drawings don't just show what the building will look like; they are capable of representing the potential reality of the building in a more complete and accurate way, including the relative sizes of its parts. This type of drawing is more like a model or 'analogue' of the building than a picture. That innocent-sounding phrase 'the relative sizes of its parts' introduces an aspect of architectural theory of enormous importance: the question of proportion. Proportion is so important that at certain times in the history of architectural theory it has threatened to take over the whole subject.

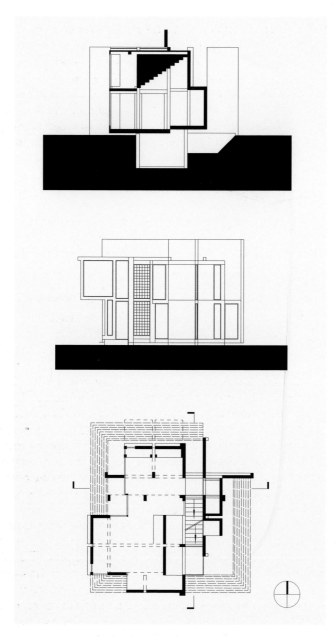

Orthographic drawings, such plans, sections and elevations (these are of House VI by Peter Eisenman, 1975) might incidentally create a visual impression, but their main purpose is to represent the building analogically. Often they are 'to scale' and can be used by a builder who may have no interest in what the building is going to look like.

Harmonic proportion

When we think about proportion we are thinking about form and the delineation of form. Most buildings are complex objects, not single forms but collections of forms. These forms are usually structural or functional – columns, beams, roofs, walls, buttresses, rooms, doors, windows and so on – but sometimes they are purely ornamental, and very often they are a mixture of the functional and the ornamental, like classical cornices and pilasters. Fitting together forms like this can be an extremely complicated business, even at a purely practical level. But of course, as architects, we want more than that; we don't just want a combination of forms that works and stands up, we want it to be beautiful. The combining of forms into beautiful wholes is one definition of architecture. Le Corbusier's version was: 'The masterly, correct, and magnificent play of forms in light'. Over the centuries, various systematic procedures have been devised to help with this difficult process, mostly by limiting the allowable combinations of forms and regulating their relative sizes. The easiest way to see how this works is to look at a simple example, such as the system advocated by Alberti in the fifteenth century. Immediately, a rather surprising aspect of the subject of proportion comes into view. In *De re aedificatoria,* Alberti wrote: 'We shall therefore borrow all our rules for the finishing of our proportions from the Musicians'.[3] Musicians? How did they get involved? It turns out that music and proportion are very closely related.

If you pluck any open string on a guitar, then stop that string at the twelfth fret and pluck it again, you will hear the musical interval known as an octave. The second note is higher than the first yet they sound somehow the same. In conventional music notation they are given the same name, even though they appear in different positions on the stave. Now measure the total length of the string, from the nut to the bridge, and the distance from the twelfth fret to the bridge – in other words the two effective lengths of the string that you plucked. You will find that the second distance is exactly half of the first. The octave therefore corresponds to the numerical ratio 1:2. If we use this ratio to draw a rectangle then the result will be a double square – a very common proportion in architecture. This is called a 'harmonic' proportion because it corresponds to a musical harmony. An octave is a special kind of harmony. If the two notes are sounded simultaneously (the musical equivalent of drawing a rectangle) they sound almost like one note. But if we play simultaneously the two notes that correspond to the ratio 2:3 or 3:4 then we hear a sweet-sounding chord. These ratios correspond to the musical intervals known as a fifth and a fourth.

Musical harmony can be 'explained' in terms of physics and mathematics – the ratios between the lengths of the strings corresponding to the ratios between the frequencies of vibrations of the strings – but science cannot easily explain the sweetness of the sound we hear. We don't need to understand the physics in order to experience the sweetness. It doesn't need to be learned, it seems already to be inside us, waiting to be awakened by musical harmony. For the philosophers, artists and architects of the Renaissance this extraordinary aspect of human experience was a sign. It meant that every part of the universe, from the revolving crystal spheres that held the stars in their places to the mind of the humblest individual human being, was governed by a harmonious system of relationships. Musical harmony was just one manifestation of a greater, cosmic harmony. Traditionally, it was the Greek philosopher and mathematician, Pythagoras who first discovered the connection between geometry and music. In the Renaissance the idea was revived by so-called 'NeoPlatonist' thinkers and pressed into the service of architecture by the pioneers of the new 'modern' (that is to say revived classical) style, such as Alberti and, before him, Filippo Brunelleschi. If we look at the church of San Lorenzo in Florence,

The church of San Lorenzo in Florence by Brunelleschi. The beautiful proportions of this interior are called 'harmonic' because they correspond to the ratios that govern musical harmony. Brunelleschi was certainly aware of this connection between the visible and the audible.

designed by Brunelleschi in the mid-fifteenth century, we find that its overall form and the elements of which is composed are regulated by those simple harmonic proportions: 1:2, 2:3 and 3:4.

But does this have anything to do with cosmic harmony? It could be just a practical expedient. After all, if one sets out a building on a square grid like a chess board, those simple harmonic rectangles are bound to appear anyway. And a building that uses round arches automatically displays the proportion 2:1 since the semicircle can be contained in a double square. Architectural historians have always argued about the real meanings of proportional systems. Some have emphasized their simple usefulness, others have read philosophical, not to say mystical, meanings into them. Proportion is not, after all, merely a question of abstract form. It has material implications. When an engineer measures the 'slenderness ratio' of a column, he or she is concerned with proportion only in so far as it affects structural stability. In this case the appearance of the column is irrelevant, although a structurally unstable column will probably look unstable and therefore be displeasing to the eye.

Gothic cathedrals like Chartres or Notre-Dame in Paris are mostly regular, well proportioned structures but we know very little about the proportional systems used by their builders. Some archaeologists and historians have found 'secret' geometries in these buildings, others have found only practical geometrical constructions used to ensure accuracy on the building site and conformity to structural rules of thumb. In an age before measuring systems were standardized, simple geometry could

As with San Lorenzo, the masons that built Notre-Dame in Paris also used simple proportional systems, but probably for practical rather than philosophical reasons.

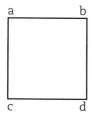
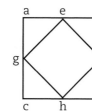
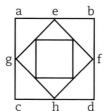
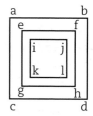

This diagram, showing the geometrical procedure known as *ad quadratum*, is adapted from a drawing by the fifteenth-century German architect Matthäus Roriczer.

at least guarantee internal consistency and regularity. For example, a mason would set out the outer wall of a cloister by drawing a square on the ground, checking that the diagonals were equal to ensure that the corners were right angles. He would then connect the mid points of the sides of the square to form a second, smaller square at 45 degrees. Turning this second square to line up with the first gave him the size and position of the inner wall or colonnade. This simple procedure, known as *ad quadratum*, may have been one of the secrets of the mason's lodge, but it hardly seems mystical now.

There is ample evidence, however, that the new breed of intellectual artist/architects of the Renaissance were well aware of concepts like harmonic proportion. They wanted their buildings to participate in that cosmic harmony that regulated the universe, including humankind. Leonardo da Vinci's famous drawing of the figure of a man inscribed within a square and a circle has architectural origins. It is called 'Vitruvian Man' because it was an illustration of a passage from Vitruvius's *De Architectura*, the only architectural treatise to survive from the ancient world. For certain Renaissance architects, the question of

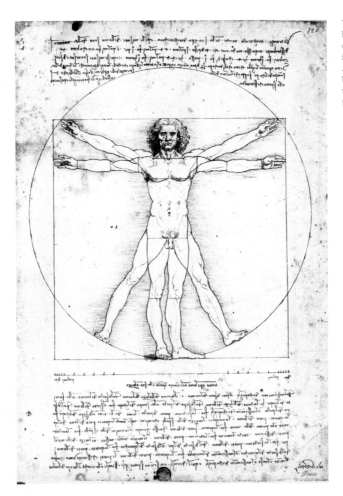

This famous drawing by Leonardo da Vinci is derived from a passage in Vitruvius's *De Architectura*, the only book about architecture to have survived from the ancient world.

proportion was not a narrow professional concern but nothing less than a reflection the nature of the universe itself, with Man at its centre.

We tend to assume that proportion in architecture is mainly a question of beauty, or as we would say these days, 'aesthetics'. A modern way of testing the relative beauty of proportional systems might be to conduct a survey: take 100 people, show them some rectangles of different proportions and see which ones they prefer. The rectangles that got the most votes would be declared the most beautiful. Such an exercise would have been utterly meaningless to the architects of the Renaissance. They sought not to separate subject from object – survey-participant from proportional system, with one passing judgment on the other – but to unite them in a single concept of harmony. The proportions of their buildings were part of the same cosmic system as the proportions of the human body. If the buildings were beautiful, it was because, like music, they awakened in the human observer the mysterious sweetness of inner harmony.

The problem of perspective

But there was a problem. Musical harmonies remained constant whereas visual harmonies were distorted by the effects of perspective. The Doppler effect – the pitch distortion caused by relative movement that

Masaccio was one of the first painters to master perfect, illusionistic perspective. In his *Trinity* of 1425, the crucifixion takes place in a barrel-vaulted Roman building. In position on the nave wall of Santa Maria Novella in Florence, it looks like a real space that you could climb into.

can be heard every time a car drives past – was almost imperceptible in an age before motorized transport. Musical harmony seemed to be audible regardless of the position of the hearer in relation to the source of the sound. Vision, though, was different. To the human eye, the forms of a building were apparently tapered and foreshortened so that their harmonious proportions were impossible to appreciate. The architects could argue, perhaps, that this was relatively unimportant. What mattered was the intrinsic, not the visible beauty of the proportions. Human beings couldn't see the beauty, but God could. The building still participated in the harmony of creation. We are already familiar with

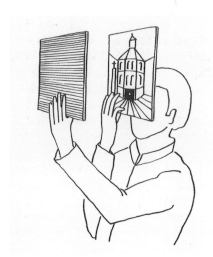

A reconstruction of the procedure used by Brunelleschi to demonstrate that his perspective system conformed to the geometry of human vision. Through a hole in the vanishing point of the drawing, the demonstrator is checking the reflection in the mirror against the direct view of the depicted building, which is the Baptistery of Florence cathedral.

this distinction between the intrinsic and the visible; it is the difference between an orthographic drawing and a perspective drawing. And it may not be a coincidence that orthographic, scale drawings began to be used in the design of buildings for the first time in the early Renaissance. The idea of intrinsic beauty, a beauty that has nothing to do with vision, seems illogical now, but we can still understand it. Architects are often perfectionists, striving for consistency and regularity in their buildings even when nobody is going to see it. These qualities are built into the very concept of architecture.

But still, from a Renaissance humanist standpoint, the seeming imperfection of human vision was frustrating. If Man stood at the centre of God's creation, hearing the earthly echoes of the music of the spheres, why was the visible manifestation of this harmony hidden from him? The difficulty was overcome in 1413 by the demonstration of a new drawing technique, the technique we now call perspective. It is perhaps surprising to learn that the method for more accurately depicting the world as human beings see it was not discovered until the early fifteenth century. The ancient Romans painted illusionistic scenes, like views through windows, on the walls of their houses. Some are preserved at Pompeii. But in these, the optical effects of distance are recreated only approximately. They lack the calculated accuracy of the true perspective. In medieval paintings the realistic depiction of three-dimensional space is of little importance. Buildings, objects and people are positioned according to their symbolic significance, or the part they play in the story being told. It is not until the early Renaissance, in pictures like Masaccio's *Trinity* of 1425, that true perspective appears for the first time. The main focus of that painting is the crucified figure of Christ, but what must have startled and amazed those that first set eyes on it is the painted building that frames the event. A Roman arch supported by Ionic columns and flanked by giant Corinthian pilasters terminates a coffered tunnel vault drawn in perfect perspective, with every coffer realistically foreshortened. When in position on the wall of the church of Santa Maria Novella in Florence, it looks like a real space you could climb into. It was not Masaccio that invented perspective, however; it was his friend Brunelleschi, who was an architect.

The account of Brunelleschi's demonstration is told by his biographer, Manetti, and has been retold many times since.[4] The essence of it is that Brunelleschi made an accurate perspective drawing of the Baptistery in Florence, as seen from the steps of the cathedral, and cut a small viewing hole in the middle of it, at the vanishing point. He then set up a mirror facing the drawing, and placed the whole contraption at the precise original viewpoint on the steps, with the drawing facing the baptistery. Anyone looking through the hole from the back of the drawing, would see the drawing reflected in the mirror and beyond it the baptistery itself. The two were seen to coincide perfectly, proving that Brunelleschi could simulate human vision accurately in a two-dimensional drawing. This skill seems unremarkable now. We expect any reasonably competent artist to be able to draw, by eye, a fairly accurate likeness of a simple building. But this is because artists have become so accustomed to perspective representations that they are able to see the real scene before them *as if it were* a perspective representation.

In fact there are a number of important differences between the perspective view and the view we actually see with our eyes. After all, we hardly ever look at views while standing perfectly still with one eye closed and the other gazing along a perfectly horizontal line. And although perspective drawings do model human vision fairly accurately, they also have features that are merely conventional. For example, buildings are commonly depicted in what is known as 'two-point' perspective, which is a radical simplification of the optical facts. We have become so used to it, however, that when we look at the theoretically more realistic three-point perspectives that computers commonly produce, they look wrong. Perhaps, as computer perspectives become more common, the convention will change and our belief in the match between drawing and reality will be restored.

Brunelleschi, of course, did not draw his view of the Baptistery by eye; he constructed it geometrically. The question is: why? The obvious answer is in order to help painters, like his friend Masaccio, to create illusionistic spatial representations like the *Trinity*. But Brunelleschi was not himself a painter; he was an architect (he originally trained as a goldsmith). Is it possible that there was some architectural motive for the demonstration, and that the benefit for painters was merely a by-product? Why would an architect want to demonstrate that the ratio of diminution of objects of equal size (in a perspective drawing, and apparently in actual human vision) is inversely proportional to their distance from the eye? As soon as we put it this way, we realize that Brunelleschi's real purpose must have been to remove that annoying objection to the concept of visual harmony. This is not the place for a detailed explanation of the geometry of perspective. Suffice it to say that the implication of the demonstration was that although the proportions of a building seemed to be distorted by the human eye, in fact they were preserved by a simple mathematical formula. So Man could appreciate visible harmonies after all. Brunelleschi had restored him once again to his place at the centre of God's creation.

A fascinating implication of this theory (and it is only a theory; not all scholars agree with it) is that architecture itself – whether real or painted – becomes a demonstration of the laws of perspective and thereby of the harmony of the universe. Perspective and architecture are mutually dependent; each needs the other to prove its proportionality. Together, they form a mechanism designed to reveal nothing less than the true nature of reality and man's place in it. In the light of this, it is easy to see Brunelleschi's own buildings – the church of Santo Spirito, for example, with its rows of identical columns, its round arches and its subtle articulations picked out in blue stone – as demonstrations of the principles of harmonic proportion in perspective.

Proportional systems

But we mustn't get carried away. Most buildings are regular and metrical to some degree, and many employ proportional systems. It doesn't necessarily make them symbols of cosmic harmony. As we have seen, proportional systems can have a purely practical purpose, like the simple geometrical constructions used by the medieval masons. An interesting feature of these systems is that, though geometrically simple, they are arithmetically rather complex. For example, the very simple geometrical procedure illustrated opposite produces a rectangle with the proportions 1:1.6180339887… The second term of this ratio is a number known as phi, which, like the better known pi, is 'irrational' and can never be absolutely determined. All sorts of extraordinary qualities have been attributed to this rectangle. It is said, for example, that of all possible rectangles it is the one most appealing to the human eye. Surveys have been conducted to prove it. And the ratio of its sides is said to be 'nature's ratio' because it seems to correspond to certain formal features of organic growth, like the spiral of a shell and the spacing of branches on the stem of a plant. The rectangle has a special name – the golden section – and it is extremely important in the history of art and architecture. Historians and archaeologists have looked for, and sometimes thought they have found, evidence of the use of the golden section in ancient buildings like the Parthenon and in medieval cathedrals. But finding proportional systems in existing buildings by measurement alone is a notoriously unreliable procedure and documentary evidence is extremely thin. In any case, why should the use of simple geometry have any symbolic importance? The golden section is very easy to construct and, as we have seen, before any national or international systems of measurement existed, it made practical sense to use geometry rather than arithmetic to decide the dimensions of a building.

So there are two basic types of proportional system: the harmonic system characteristic of Renaissance architecture, and the geometric system, which may or may not have been used in the ancient and medieval periods. The former is 'commensurate', which means that it consists essentially of rectangles formed by whole numbers of squares, and the latter is 'irrational' because, although simple to construct, it produces awkward and unwieldy numbers. Both systems claim to reveal hidden aspects of nature or cosmology, but both also have simple practical functions on the building site. To our modern, instrumental way of thinking, it is those practical functions that matter most. Cosmic harmony and the imitation of nature are less important, though these ideas have not been entirely forgotten, as we shall see.

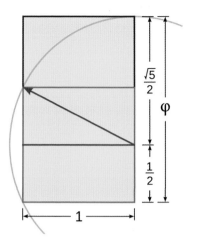 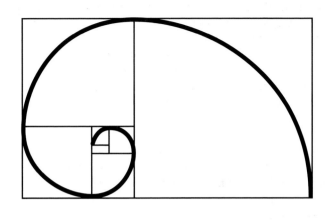

The so-called golden section (left) has long been thought to have mystical properties, partly because one of the terms in its ratio is the irrational number phi. But if the arithmetic associated with the golden section is rather complex, the geometry used to construct it is extremely simple. When we find golden sections in ancient architecture we may be discovering nothing more mysterious than a mason's practical rule of thumb. The Fibonacci series can be represented as an expanding spiral of squares (right) that reflects natural growth forms.

Modular co-ordination

One modern descendant of the traditional proportional systems was what was called, in the middle years of the twentieth century, 'modular co-ordination'. When Henry Ford set up the first moving assembly line for cars in 1913, he established mass production as the industrial and economic theme of the century. Almost immediately, progressive architects like Walter Gropius began to ask why buildings such as ordinary houses could not be cheaply mass-produced like cars.[5] Fordist mass production inevitably meant standardization. The secret of a more efficient building industry therefore lay, thought Gropius, in the standardization of building components. Walls, floors, roofs, windows, doors – all could be mass produced in factories to standard sizes and quickly assembled on site to make a range of different buildings. The key thing was to co-ordinate the dimensions of the components so that they would fit snugly together. They would need to be sized in multiples of a given basic dimension or 'module'. When an architect designed a building, he or she would use only the approved modular dimensions. In effect, they would be designing on a standard grid, so why not just draw the grid on the paper first and allow it to dictate the overall dimensions of the building? Well, this of course was nothing new. Architects had been drawing grids of one kind or another for centuries without the spur of mass production. Standardization and repetition were normal characteristics of most architecture, and sophisticated systems had already been devised to co-ordinate dimensions.

In the 1950s and 1960s, modular co-ordination became almost a religion among those architects who designed houses and schools for the post-war welfare society. They mostly ignored the traditional proportional systems, preferring simple grids of squares, commonly based on a 100-millimetre (4-inch) module. Efficiency was the aim, not beauty. Even so, the advantages of modular co-ordination eventually turned out to be something of a myth. Industrialized building campaigns, like the famous Hertfordshire schools programme of the 1950s, in the end proved to be no more efficient than traditional construction. For many good, practical reasons, the building industry stubbornly refused

to model itself on the car industry. Ironically, now that twentieth-century mass production has been replaced by twenty-first-century 'mass customization', it could be argued that the car industry is becoming more like the building industry, making bespoke products in small batches.[6]

But not all architects of the mid-century were prepared to see the ancient mysteries of proportion reduced to mere production engineering. Among the more intellectual members of the profession, proportion became a major topic for theoretical discussion with the publication in 1949 of *Architectural Principles in the Age of Humanism* by Rudolf Wittkower. The book gives what is still the clearest and most convincing elucidation of the history and theory of Renaissance proportion, in particular its musical or harmonic basis. Progressive architects like Alison and Peter Smithson welcomed it because it gave them an excuse, now that the initial iconoclastic stage of Modernism had passed, to interest themselves once again in architectural history. The principles of proportion were as relevant to modern buildings as they were to classical ones. The critic Colin Rowe, in the now famous essay 'The Mathematics of the Ideal Villa' published in 1947, had shown how Le Corbusier's Villa Stein-de Monzie of 1927 – already an icon of the Modernist style – displayed the same overall proportions as Palladio's Villa Foscari of 1550–60. Suddenly history, and proportion, were back, including the idea that a building might echo the harmony of the cosmos. But of course, as Rowe's essay proved, this was not news to Le Corbusier.

The Modulor

Le Corbusier was never afraid to think, talk, write and design in terms as grand as 'cosmic harmony'. Proportion had always fascinated him. His most famous book *Vers une architecture* (*Towards a New Architecture*), published in 1923, contains photographs of the facades of old buildings with diagonal lines drawn on them to prove that they are composed of similar rectangles. In the late 1940s, he finally got round to devising his own proportional system, which he called the Modulor, a contraction of *module d'or*, meaning golden module. The Modulor was going to be the system to end all systems. It would, he was sure, become the standard method for determining the dimensions of buildings all over the world. Naturally, it was based on the golden section, the most ancient and prestigious of all ratios. If nature used the golden section, then so

Colin Rowe, in an influential essay of 1947, found proportional similarities between Le Corbusier's Villa Stein-de Monzie (plan and elevation below) and Palladio's Villa Foscari (right). Rowe's essay and others like it helped to re-introduce history and theory into the world of architectural practice at a time when the profession was in thrall to a purely instrumental industrial culture.

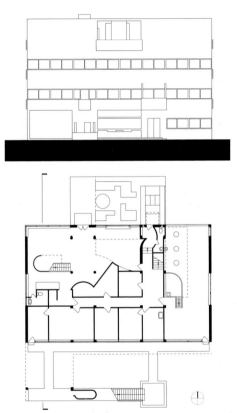

would Le Corbusier. He realized, however, that choosing a geometrically constructed rectangle meant that he would have to find some way of coping with irrational numbers. It was all very well for medieval masons to set out their buildings using only knotted strings, but the modern building industry needed scale drawings and consistent dimensions. It needed arithmetic, not geometry. Le Corbusier found the answer to this problem in the so-called Fibonacci series, a sequence of simple numbers in which each number is the sum of the previous two. For example: 1,1,2,3,5,8,13,21 and so on.

This was the arithmetic equivalent of an expanding spiral of squares that seems to reflect natural growing forms. But a single Fibonacci series would be too coarse and inflexible to be useful as an architectural scale, so Le Corbusier added a second scale, which was simply a doubling of the first, thus: 2, 2, 4, 6, 10, 16, 26, 42. The combination of these two scales, designated red and blue, provided the extra refinement and flexibility needed. Faced with any detailed design problem – a room with doors, windows and built-in furniture, say – an architect could decide the dimensions all of the necessary components using only the fixed divisions of the double Fibonacci sequence. In theory, all the dimensions would be related proportionately to the golden section.

The Modulor therefore overcame the geometry-versus-arithmetic problem, combining the mystique of the golden section with the practical advantages of a standard scale. But if it was going to conquer the world and populate it with beautifully proportioned buildings, it would need to find some accommodation with existing systems of measurement, like the metric and imperial systems. An early metric version of the scale proved unwieldy, resulting in too few handy whole numbers, but when the scale was translated into feet and inches, which was then the standard system in Britain and is still the standard system in America, everything fell into place. 'To our delight,' says Le Corbusier in his book on the Modulor, 'the graduations of a new Modulor, based on a man six feet tall, translated themselves into round figures in feet and inches.'[7]

We have now come to the most important aspect of the Modulor: that 6-foot (1.83-metre) tall man. Like his Renaissance predecessors, Le Corbusier saw his proportional system not just as a tool but as a revelatory model of the universe and Man's place in it. If the Modulor was to fulfil its potential, it would have to be based not just on an abstract geometrical figure but also on the dimensions of the human body. Le Corbusier of course knew about Vitruvian Man. His version inscribes the human figure not in a square and a circle, but in a golden section, or rather a combination of squares and golden sections. The key dimensions are from the foot to the navel, from the navel to the top of the head and from the top of the head to the fingertips of the raised arm. This turns out to be a Fibonacci series.

The importance of scale

Modulor Man is the twentieth-century symbol of an old and important theme in architectural theory: the question of scale. At one level, it is a purely practical matter. Buildings are mostly designed for people to use, so it makes sense to size them accordingly. Rooms must be the right size for the human activities they accommodate, doors must be big enough to walk through, window sills must be low enough to see out of, and so on. Of course, not all buildings are purely functional. Some have symbolic meanings of which scale is an aspect. It is very common, for example, for doors in monumental buildings to be much taller than is strictly necessary for a person to pass through. This is a sign. It means that the building is an important one and that this is its main entrance. In this case scale becomes not a practical but an aesthetic and linguistic matter.

In the context of proportion, the question of scale inevitably leads

Le Corbusier not only studied proportion but invented a whole new system of his own. Called the Modulor, it used the Fibonacci number series, which is detectable in certain natural forms like spiral shells (see page 57), to arrive at a fixed range of preferred dimensions. 'Modulor Man' was le Corbusier's answer to 'Vitruvian Man'.

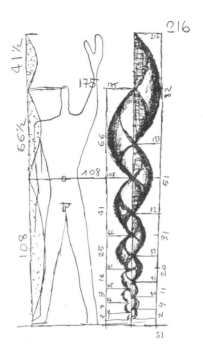

to a discussion about dimensions in general and how they are arrived at. Take the imperial system of feet and inches, for example. The very words betray the origins of the system in the human body. A foot is the length of a foot, an inch is the length of the last joint of the thumb (the French word '*pouce*' means both inch and thumb), a yard is the length of a pace, or alternatively the length of a man's outstretched arm measured from the middle of his body – and so on. In ancient times and in the Middle Ages, when there were no standardized measuring systems, the human body itself was the standard. The metric system now used by the building industries of European and other countries has no basis in the human body. It was fixed by the French Academy of Sciences in 1791 at 1/10,000,000 of the distance from the Equator to the North Pole measured through Paris. Nevertheless, in the theory and practice of architecture, the idea that there should be some discernible relationship between the dimensions of the human body and the dimensions of a building persists. But how is this relationship perceived? Can the soaring, vertiginous interior of a medieval cathedral really be said to bear any dimensional relationship to the human figures that it dwarfs? If it does, then it must be through the smaller parts of which it is composed: the rhythm of the arcades and the bays of the vaulting, the division into levels or storeys, the hierarchies of windows, and the niches which, like miniature buildings, house the sculptural representations of human figures. And if all of these elements are related to each other proportionately, then the whole space, however vast, becomes a human space. In short, it becomes architecture.

CHAPTER 4
SPACE

It is time to think about architectural space – its origins, its meaning and its human qualities. When we use the word 'space' we think we know exactly what we mean. For the eighteenth-century philosopher Immanuel Kant, space, like time, was 'a priori', which means roughly 'already given'. What he meant was that the world is unimaginable without space, so there is no point trying to prove its existence. It is a precondition for the existence of everything. Later developments in cosmology, from Einstein's theory of relativity to string theory, may have cast some doubt on this proposition, but in ordinary human experience it remains true enough. In the modern world view, space is everywhere. It extends infinitely in all directions, with nothing left over and nothing excluded from it. We may not be able to inhabit much of this space, but nevertheless we think of it as potentially inhabitable. We human beings have visited some of the very nearest parts of outer space and in principle, with a little help from technology, we may one day visit more of it. We might even venture beyond our solar system. The makers of *Star Trek* have already imagined 'warp drive'; all that remains is for someone to engineer it. In our minds, despite what the cosmologists try to tell us about space-time, space has three dimensions: height, width and depth. We can fix the position of any object in space by specifying these co-ordinates in relation to some fixed point, such as our own location. Space can be cluttered up with objects or filled by substances, whether solid, liquid or gas, but conceptually it is empty – a vacuum. If asked 'what is space' this is how most of us would describe it – as an infinite void.

This hasn't always been the standard answer, though. In medieval European thought, for example, space was not infinite, could never be a void, and did not extend uniformly in all directions. There were different kinds of space. Terrestrial space, the space in which we live, was just one region of a universe that included at least two other, completely different kinds of space called Heaven and Hell, one located beyond the outermost of the crystal spheres to which the stars were fixed, the other deep in the bowels of the earth. Not even committed Christians now think of Heaven and Hell as parts of the real universe. They are thought of as different kinds of existence, spiritual as opposed to bodily, rather than different kinds of space. But even terrestrial space was perceived differently in the Middle Ages. Medieval philosophers, following Artistotle, thought of space only in relation to material objects or masses. Space was what contained these masses, like a jug containing water. Spaces were therefore more like surfaces than volumes, and the whole universe was filled with them, all nested tightly together – the water within the jug, the jug within the air, the air within the room, the room within the house, the house within the outer air contained by the first of the celestial spheres. We now find it quite hard to visualize space this way, so accustomed have we become to thinking of it as an infinite void. But Aristotle and his medieval followers found it equally hard to grasp the concepts of 'infinity' and 'void'.

Medieval and Renaissance space

The transition from a medieval to a modern concept of space can best be appreciated by looking at late medieval and early Renaissance paintings. Take, for example, the main panel of Duccio's *Maestà* altarpiece, painted for Siena Cathedral in about 1310. The Virgin and Child are enthroned in the middle of the picture and attended by a company of saints and angels arranged in rows on either side. In one sense, all of these figures obviously occupy the same space. The saints are almost within touching distance of the Virgin and their worshiping gestures are directed at her. But in another sense they can't possibly be in the same space unless the Virgin is a giant, since she seems to be about twice the size of the saints. Her size is dictated not by her position in the space but by her importance in the story. She occupies a different space within the same picture. In other words, the space in the painting is discontinuous and generated by the figures and objects in the picture. Now look at another panel in the same altarpiece, the one depicting the 'second annunciation', or announcement of the Virgin's death. At first this painting seems spatially more unified. There is no difference of scale between the Virgin and the announcing angel and they seem to occupy an actual room with solid walls and architectural features such as arched doorways. But the unity is not quite perfect. We might allow a supernatural being in a painting to hover a few inches above the floor, but should the bench on which the Virgin sits also be hovering? When we pay attention to these details, it begins to seem that the figures do not after all occupy the space of the room. It is almost as if they have been cut out of another picture and pasted on.

In most Gothic and Byzantine art, different objects are allowed to occupy different spaces (and also different times) in the same painting. Spatial unity is not important. It is symbolism that counts. But in the paintings of Duccio, Giotto and Cimabue, symbolism is becoming less important as a determinant of composition, and space is beginning to take priority. We seem to be witnessing the emergence of the modern concept of space as an infinite void extending uniformly in all directions.

The medieval world contained different kinds of space, including Heaven and Hell as well as the Earth and the visible cosmos, as depicted in this *Last Judgement* by Giotto in the Scrovegni Chapel, Padua (c.1305).

Perfect spatial unity in painting was not finally achieved until more than 100 years later, when the architect Filippo Brunelleschi worked out the geometrical principles of perspective representation. Painting would never be the same again. More importantly, the modern concept of space as a continuous void came suddenly into focus. If it could be represented convincingly in painting, if it could be grasped and manipulated, then its full significance could be appreciated. Look at Piero della Francesca's *Flagellation of Christ*, painted in the 1450s. It is a mysterious, disturbing painting, and at first its composition seems anything but unified. The three figures on the right (probably the Duke of Urbino and his advisors) seem remote, both temporally and spatially, from the curiously still violence of the biblical event taking place in the background under a pristine classical canopy. That architectural setting is important, especially the perfectly adjusted perspective pattern of the paving, because it makes it clear to us that the apparent difference in size between the figures on the right and figures on the left is caused by their different positions in the depth of the painting. We are looking not at a collection of spaces generated by a collection of figures and objects but at a single unified space in which objects and figures are arranged. And this is not just a space but *the* space, the infinite void extending uniformly in all directions. We are looking at the scene through a picture frame as we would look through a window at the real world.

Duccio's *Maestà* altarpiece (1308–11). Do these figures occupy the same space? If so then the Virgin is a giant. Her size is in proportion to her symbolic importance rather than to the people and objects around her. Perhaps, then, she occupies a different space – possible in the Middle Ages, impossible now.

In this depiction of the second annunciation from the same altarpiece, space is more unified and therefore more like the space we are used to now – but should the Virgin's bench be floating in the air like that? Consistent perspective had yet to be invented.

Piero's *Flagellation of Christ* (1450s) is a very strange painting. Its divided focus, its curious combination of stillness and violence, and its contrasting scales make it appear fragmented. But its space is unified by the recently invented system of perspective.

Architectural space

What has the infinite void got to do with architecture? Is it a useful
concept? Is architectural space – the space inside a room, for example –
really nothing more than a slice cut out of universal space? Somehow,
in our everyday experience of actual architectural spaces, this seems
an inadequate description. The space inside a room has specific
qualities that universal space lacks, qualities like enclosure, direction,
orientation and scale. This room that we find ourselves in probably has
four walls, a floor and a ceiling. If we were to make a model of the room
in cardboard or on a computer, then these enclosing elements might
be indistinguishable one from another. How could we tell, for example,
which was the floor and which the ceiling? But in the real room we are
in no doubt because this particular slice of universal space happens to
be resting on the surface of a planet and is therefore subject to gravity.
It has an up and a down, and we experience that difference the way we
experience everything else in the world, through our bodies and minds.
This may seem too obvious to require comment, but it makes clear a very
important difference between space as conceptualized by science – the
infinite void – and space as experienced by human beings.

It is dangerous to generalize about 'science' – of which there
are many different kinds – but traditionally scientists treat the world
as an object to be observed and measured. They separate themselves
from the world in order to view it 'objectively', and they do not allow
human nature to influence their findings. This method is artificial and
in a sense unreal, since the mind of the scientist is inevitably part of
a human body, and that body is inevitably a part of the world that is
being observed. The idea that it might be separated from the world is a
kind of necessary fiction, an untruth accepted as a starting point for the
pursuit of a different kind of truth. But human beings, when they are not
being scientists, do not look at the world objectively. They always see it
in relation to themselves, their bodies, their minds and the bodies and
minds of other human beings. Those philosophers who call themselves
'phenomenologists' are more interested in this everyday relationship
between the human being and world than in the objectivity of science.
It is no surprise that phenomenology has been influential in the theory
of architecture, which modifies parts of the world in order that human
beings might inhabit them. When an architect thinks about space, he
or she is thinking about a relationship, not an objective phenomenon –
human space, not scientific space.

So, we are in an ordinary room and the space in that room, like the
space in all ordinary rooms, has an up and a down. It is not generalized
and uniform, but specific and differentiated. We experience the
difference between up and down through our bodies. Very occasionally
we stand on our heads but most of the time we do what evolution on
this planet designed us to do, and stand on our feet. The architectural
details of a room will sometimes acknowledge this fact, treating the floor
and ceiling differently and echoing the standing human figure in, for
example, columns with bases and capitals. The space in the room might
be directional in other ways. For example, its plan might be rectangular
rather than square or circular. Once again, we experience this slight
spatial irregularity through our bodies and with reference to what

our bodies are capable of. We might think of it in terms of an implied movement, a movement that we can enact by walking from one end of the room to the other. When we reach the far end of the room we will no doubt turn and face the room again so as to get a better view of it. The architecture of the room might encourage us to do this, presenting itself to our view in the same way that we present ourselves to the view of other human beings. Perhaps the view from one end of the room is more important than the view from the other. The view from the entrance, for example, might be especially important because this is where we gain our first impression. So our room is now differentiated in more ways than simple up and down; it has sides and ends, a near and a far, a place of entry and a place of destination, a front and a back, and we experience these differences through our bodies for which they are the means of orientation.

The phenomenological approach

The architecture of the room is profoundly influenced by the 'architecture' of the human body and of human experience. A room is an interior and 'interiority', except in very exceptional circumstances such as out-of-body sensations, is a continuous human experience. We seem to live inside our bodies, looking out at the world through our eyes. Looking at an actual room, we see a reflection of this constant human experience of interiority. We might even be prompted to decorate the room with thoughts and dreams. When we think of architectural space in this phenomenological way, common features like doors and windows become much more than just functional arrangements; they become symbols of human experience, of our confinement in our bodies and of our freedom to explore the world, of our introversion and our extraversion.

In a book called *The Poetics of Space*, written in 1958 by the French philosopher Gaston Bachelard, the author conducts a phenomenological analysis of a traditional French urban house such as the one in which he grew up. The house, for Bachelard, is a kind of model of human experience, a home for the mind as well as the body, and especially a home for dreams. He says: 'The house shelters daydreaming, the house protects the dreamer, the house allows one to dream in peace.' Certain parts of the house correspond to certain types of dream. The attic, with its clear, functional shape, its views over the city and its visible carpentry, is home to the rational thought of the daylight hours. In the cellar, on the other hand, lurk the mysteries of the subconscious and the irrational fears of the night. 'It is first and foremost the dark entity of the house, the one that partakes of subterranean forces. When we dream there, we are in harmony with the irrationality of the depths.'[1] These associations are familiar to us from poetry and literature. One might say that they are conventional. But that is why they are important – because the space we actually experience, as opposed to the space of objective reality, is profoundly cultural. It is a human construct. Architects, no matter how rational they think they are, inevitably deal in the poetry as well as the science of space.

In an essay entitled 'Building, Dwelling, Thinking', delivered as a lecture in 1951, the German philosopher Martin Heidegger uses an architectural example – an old farmhouse in the Black Forest – to illustrate that most fundamental of human experiences, the experience of 'dwelling'.[2] Heidegger is concerned with the question of being. It would be hard to imagine a more important topic for philosophy. And yet, on its own, this word 'being', which can be both a verb and a noun, is rather hard to deal with because we can't imagine being without being *somewhere*. All beings, including human beings, need somewhere to be, and this 'being somewhere' is what Heidegger calls dwelling. He points out that the old German word for dwelling, *Buan*, is the root of the modern word for building, *Bauen*. So dwelling and building are in some sense the same. What's more, they are inseparable from thinking itself, the very activity in which, as a philosopher, Heidegger is engaged. Thought itself seems in some essential way to be spatial and structural, just like architecture. It is spatial and structural because it is the expression of beings who can only experience and understand the world through their spatial and structural bodies. The objective world proposed by science probably exists, but we can never know for sure. The only world that we can know directly is the subjective world of our bodies and minds, the world of our dwelling, and it is this world that architecture shapes and modifies.

Modern space

In this discussion of human space we have been thinking mainly about traditional buildings with rooms, attics and cellars. But what about modern space? Not all buildings have rooms, and interiority is only one among many qualities of architectural space. Twentieth century Modernist architects often seemed to want to abolish interiority altogether and replace it with a new kind of space that was neither interior nor exterior. In most buildings, for ordinary practical reasons such as weather tightness and security, it was possible to seal off the interior from the exterior by closing the doors and windows. Mies van der Rohe's Barcelona Pavilion of 1929 – so often used to epitomize the Modernist attitude to space – has no doors or windows to close. Its walls of glass and polished stone, its slender chrome-clad columns and its thin flat roof plane do not so much enclose space, keeping it locked up in a box, as let it wander around freely, never having to commit itself to being either internal or external. How does this work in phenomenological terms?

Perhaps the answer lies in the words that we use to describe this architecture – words like 'open', 'free' and 'flowing'. If the architecture of rooms corresponds to the human need for a home, a home that holds us the way that our bodies hold our minds, then Modernist space corresponds to the human need to escape from that home, to go off and explore the world. There is a paradox here. Buildings are mostly fixed, permanent structures yet they can represent freedom and escape. Architecture has the power to transcend its own nature just as we, in our imagination, transcend the limitations of our bodies.

Building types

The Barcelona Pavilion is an almost functionless building, a purely symbolic and ceremonial structure, but most buildings house everyday

The Barcelona Pavilion
by Mies van der Rohe
is the most famous
example of dynamic
modern, or 'Modernist',
space. There are no
defined rooms, not even
a definite distinction
between inside and
outside. Space is open,
free and flowing.

human activities. We tend to classify buildings according to the types
of activity they house and we expect the spaces in those buildings to
accommodate and support the activities. In 1976, the architectural
historian Nikolaus Pevsner wrote a book called *A History of Building
Types* that was organized on the basis of this classification system. There
are chapters on government buildings, theatres, libraries, museums,
hotels, shops, factories and so on. It is a characteristically Modernist view
of architectural history. Many twentieth-century Modernist architects
believed that the function of a building, in the sense of its human
use, could be defined rather precisely and that the building should be
designed to fit that function. The detailed analysis of function would,
it was hoped, produce new forms and a new architecture, free from
historical precedent. The idea is especially clear in the work of architects
like Hugo Häring, Hans Scharoun and Alvar Aalto who, unlike Mies van
der Rohe or the early Le Corbusier, rejected machine-like regularity in
favour of freer, more organic forms, tailored to human activities. Look, for
example, at Scharoun's famous Philharmonie concert hall in Berlin. Its
foyers and circulation spaces are angled and shaped to follow the natural
flow of arriving concert-goers, leaving their coats in the cloakrooms and
pausing in small groups before filtering into the hall itself. When they
enter the hall and locate their seats, they will find themselves in one of
many little sub-auditoria, each clearly defined and uniquely angled, so
that the concert-goers can almost imagine they are listening to the music
with a group of friends rather than an anonymous metropolitan crowd.
Here the architecture is not just fitting its function but responding subtly
to patterns of human use, including their psychological dimensions.

According to Pevsner's functionalist version of history, architecture
in the west developed in response to changing social patterns and
institutions. As new institutions emerged – government bureaucracies,
museums, hospitals, railway stations – new types of building were
invented to accommodate them. But curiously, as the story unfolds,

In the foyers of Hans Scharoun's Philharmonie concert hall in Berlin, space is tailored to fit the flow and rhythm of the arriving and departing concert-goers as shown in this plan. Rectilinearity and symmetry are rejected because they are still and abstract rather than dynamic and human.

In the auditorium of the Philharmonie, space is shaped to the psychological as well as the physical needs of its users. A collection of sub-auditoria creates an impression of intimacy, a sharing of the musical experience with a small number of fellow listeners.

invention turns out to be less important than continuity and tradition. Take, for example, the history of the hospital. As Pevsner points out, the words hospital, hostel, hospice and hotel all come from the Latin word *hospes*, meaning guest or host. In the early history of the hospital, it is hard to separate the idea of looking after the sick from the broader idea of 'hospitality'. In a typical medieval monastery, the sleeping quarters for visiting pilgrims were architecturally very similar to the hospital or 'infirmary', and both seemed to borrow their form from chapels and churches. Beds were ranged on either side of a long, aisled space leading to an altar. Jumping 500 years, it is not hard to detect the survival of this form in the hospital ward plan favoured by the founder of modern

This medieval diagrammatic plan of a monastery very clearly expresses very clearly the idea that buildings take particular forms according to the functions they house. But those forms develop a life of their own, surviving long after the original function has changed and being adapted to other functions.

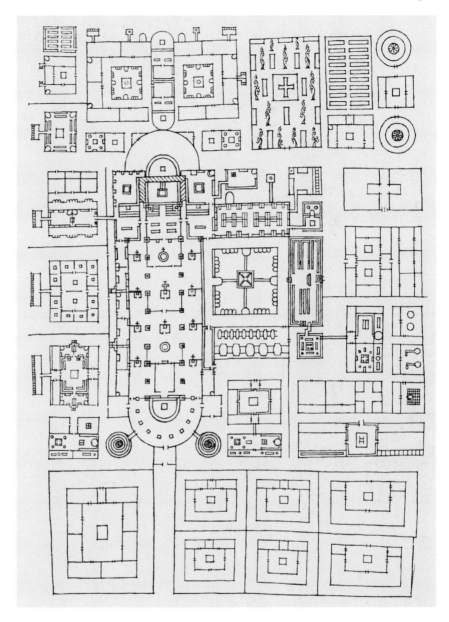

nursing, Florence Nightingale. By the late nineteenth century, the plans of hospitals had taken on an almost machine-like rationality, with Nightingale ward blocks arranged in parallel rows, or sometimes radially, in order to simplify circulation and drainage while optimizing ventilation and daylight. So although these arrangements were apparently dictated by function, nevertheless they were based on a traditional prototype.

Similar plans were adopted for mental asylums, in which patients were restrained as well as looked after. And immediately we think also of the nineteenth-century prison, in which the ward block becomes the cell block, but the overall plan is very similar. Nightingale wards are out of favour now. The patient, especially in a private hospital, is more likely to be accommodated in a separate room. But what is this if not a hotel room with added medical facilities? We are back with that original

concept of hospitality and the accommodation of visitors. So building types are less distinctly defined than we commonly assume. Hospitals, asylums, prisons and hotels belong together in a group and the boundaries between them are not always clear. We could add more types to the group: orphanages, public schools, barracks, old people's homes.

Another thing that we learn from the history of the hospital is that certain architectural forms, such as long aisled halls or 'basilicas', tend to survive and be adapted to suit new functions. (We think of the basilica as the commonest form of Christian church in the west but it was originally a secular Roman building where it combined the functions of law court and market.) New building types employing novel architectural forms are rather rare. In fact, looking at architecture from an urban point of view, the whole business of designing for specific functions – the Pevsnerian classification of buildings by functional type – looks questionable. Aldo Rossi, in his book *The Architecture of the City*, calls it 'naïve functionalism'. For him, typology is indeed an important aspect of architecture, but it has more to do with form than function. In his view an apartment block, for example, is defined as a building type not because of its residential function but because it is a common form of multi-storey, cellular structure that forms the 'background architecture' of the traditional city. Other types might include basilica, the centralized, domed structure, the tower, the pavilion, the inward-looking courtyard building, and so on. These types are traditional – handed down rather than invented – and they take their place naturally in the traditional city, the city of memory, the city in which the relationship between form and function is rather loose and provisional.

Certain built forms endure long after the functions for which they were designed have become obsolete. Take Bedford Square in London, for example. It was designed in the eighteenth century to house wealthy families and their servants but no one lives there now. The tall terraced houses, which together form palace-like fronts facing the garden, are occupied by offices, professional institutions and even a school of architecture. An architect designing new buildings to suit these functions would be very unlikely to choose the form of a terrace of tall town houses, and yet the square looks much the same as it always has. In this case, an urban form has outlived the economic, social and technological conditions that produced it, but it has not fallen into ruin because we are

Strangeways Prison, Manchester (1869; left) and University College Hospital (1906; right) in London, both designed by Alfred Waterhouse. It is hard to tell which is which. As building types, prisons and hospitals are very close to each other with a shared ancestor in the dormitories, hostels and infirmaries of the medieval monastery.

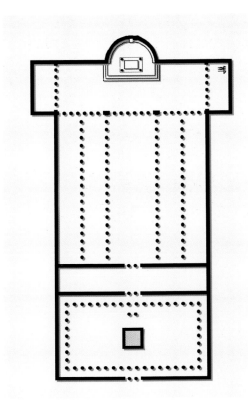

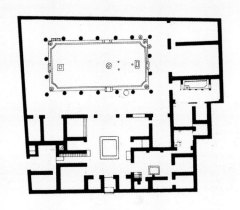

Ancient building types like the basilica (left; this plan shows the old St Peter's in Rome) and the courtyard house (right) still survive as what we might now call 'design strategies'. They can be adapted to many different functions and can be justified in purely practical terms, but respect for tradition also contributes to their vigour and longevity.

willing to live with it and accommodate our lives to it. The buildings have undergone many internal changes – making doorways in party walls to create suites of offices, for example – but Bedford Square is still Bedford Square. And the same thing is happening all over the city. Old buildings are being converted to new uses – houses into offices, factories into loft apartments, cinemas into pubs, churches into concert halls. Sometimes the old buildings are preserved because we have grown to love them and we can't bear to tear them down, sometimes they are preserved just because converting them is cheaper than building new ones.

Architecture and society

When we talk about functional types we are often referring to the institutions housed rather than the buildings designed to accommodate them. The structures of architecture reflect the structures of society, and architecture, as traditionally conceived, is always the servant of authority. When Michel Foucault sought a concrete example to illustrate his theories about the essentially disciplinary nature of western society, he chose an architectural project, the Panopticon, a form of prison invented by the utilitarian philosopher Jeremy Bentham.[3] In the Panopticon project, the rationality of the nineteenth-century hospital/asylum/prison plan is taken to its logical conclusion. The building is circular in plan, with cells around the perimeter, each visible in its entirety from a central supervisory position. The supervisor can always see all of the inmates, but the inmates can never see the supervisor. They cannot even know whether he is present or not, so they must always obey the rules in case he is. It is the nineteenth-century equivalent of the CCTV installation.

Here it serves as a particularly clear example of the way that architectural design gives form not just to the functional requirements of an institution, but also to society's values and power structures. As we have seen, building types with different names – hospital, asylum, prison – are often almost interchangeable architecturally. The difference is not in the buildings but in the labels we attach to them. The same applies at the level of detailed planning. In a complex institutional building such as a school, the spaces designed by the architect are given names that correspond to activities specified in the client's brief: classroom, assembly hall, staff room and so on. But these are just names. If, for some reason, the school becomes redundant but the need arises for a sports centre, then the building might serve this new purpose very well without much modification. Classrooms would become training rooms, the assembly hall would become the basketball court and the staff room would be turned into a coffee bar. Perhaps the Modernist emphasis on functional design – the fitting of forms precisely to patterns of human use – is unrealistic because it is too static. What is the point of drawing up detailed briefs, including floor areas and equipment schedules for specific functions, if we know that long before the building wears out those functions will have changed? It might make more sense to design simple buildings that meet the basic requirements of a broad range of activities and then change the labels as the institutional functions shift and evolve. This is the opposite of the approach adopted by Häring, Aalto and Scharoun, and it results in architecture of a very different character.

Bedford Square in London no longer serves the function for which it was designed. Town houses for aristocrats have become offices for publishers and homes for cultural institutions, including a school of architecture. The form survives intact because it is loved and remembered.

The Illinois State Penitentiary at Stateville is a panopticon prison of the type invented by Jeremy Bentham. It expresses its function like a perfect diagram. All of the prisoners in the radiating cells are visible from the supervision point in the centre. If the supervisor remains concealed he doesn't even have to be present at his post to control the behaviour of the inmates.

The National Gallery in Berlin by Mies van der Rohe is right next door to Hans Scharoun's Philharmonie and was built at about the same time. They could not be more different. In the Gallery space there is a given abstraction that function must colonize. The result is less tailored but more flexible.

Just a few hundred yards from Scharoun's Philharmonie in Berlin (see page 70) stands the German National Gallery, designed in the 1960s by Mies van der Rohe. Its function is very different, of course, and one might argue that the spatial needs of an art gallery are simpler than those of a concert hall. But nevertheless these two roughly contemporary buildings represent radically different approaches to the relationship between space and function. The National Gallery is a temple-like steel and glass structure, roughly square on plan, standing on a stone-clad podium and enclosing a single space interrupted only by a pair of lift

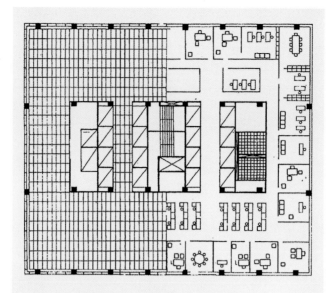

Plan of a typical floor in an office tower. It is conceived as an open, serviced space, capable of being divided in different ways to suit different occupants. The shell and core of the building are designed to last but the partitions, furniture and internal landscaping have relatively short lives.

shafts and staircases. The space serves as a grand entrance hall and houses temporary exhibitions. Permanent exhibitions are downstairs in the mostly windowless podium, which they share with ancillary spaces such as offices and toilets. The building is a monument to twentieth century western culture (when it was built, West Berlin was an island in communist East Germany) but it is also an abstract statement of an architectural principle: the principle of loose fit and functional flexibility.

Managing form and function

That same principle is routinely applied to a more mundane building type – the modern office block. Office interiors are commonly divided into two types: the cellular and the open plan, and most are a mixture of the two. It's a familiar scene: important people have rooms of their own and less important people share a room with several colleagues. Sometimes that shared office is hardly a room at all, but a whole floor of the building, divided up by furniture and free-standing screens. Cellular offices tend to occupy the best positions in the building, close to the perimeter where they have the benefit of natural light and views out, while the lower orders, especially in a 'deep-plan' building like the typical New York skyscraper, are consigned to the artificially lit, viewless interior. In architectural terms, this class distinction is perhaps less important than the overall concept of flexibility. The partitions that enclose the cellular offices will certainly be demountable so that when changes occur in the staffing of the organization, or when a new organization takes a lease on the building, everything can be rearranged and the balance between cellular and open plan can be altered.

So the fabric of the building is of two kinds: the relatively permanent structure, external envelope and services network, and the relatively temporary internal fit-out. A more radical version of this idea is the 'omniplatz' – an open, flexible, highly serviced zone in which, in theory, anything can happen anywhere. The best early example of this is the Centre Pompidou in Paris, the building that established the global

The Centre Pompidou in Paris (opposite) is the ultimate flexible building. The section and plan show how completely uninterrupted expanses of floor the size of sports fields can be adapted to almost any function. In order to achieve this, all service elements, such as escalators and air conditioning ducts, are pushed to the perimeter where they become the external expression of the building.

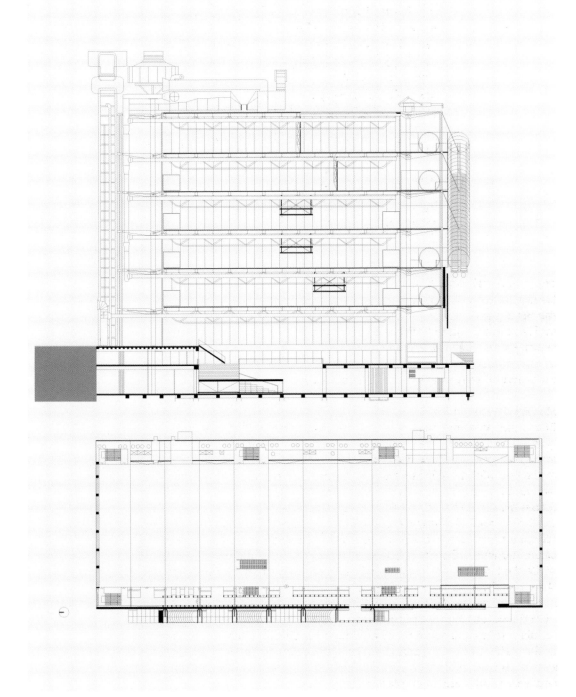

credibility of the so-called High Tech style in the 1970s. Everybody knows that the exterior of the Centre Pompidou is festooned with coloured pipes and ducts, including a long snake-like escalator tube on the side facing the piazza. All the structural elements and services installations that would normally be tucked away out of sight inside the building

Can there be architecture without buildings? Louis Kahn argued that certain social situations – a teacher and a class, for example – were archetypal and should be respected in the spatial organization of buildings.

The Salk Institute in California by Louis Kahn mainly consists of large, flexible laboratory spaces. However, most photographs of the building feature these little 'houses' which accommodate the private study spaces of the researchers. Deep thought requires solitude and privacy. The study, like the classroom, is an archetypal space.

have been banished to the exterior in order to create vast areas of uninterrupted but highly serviced floor space. The various activities or functions that the building accommodates – libraries, art galleries, theatres, cinemas, concert halls, restaurants – can, in theory, be set up anywhere and if necessary moved around without making expensive and disruptive alterations to the permanent parts of the building. Different versions of this basic idea occur in countless late twentieth-century buildings.

The American architect Louis Kahn, who had the knack of encapsulating architectural ideas in memorable phrases, talked about 'served and servant spaces'.[4] The served spaces were where the main human activities took place, and the servant spaces were the lifts, staircases, ducts, toilets and plant rooms necessary to make them usable.

This is very clearly expressed in the Richards Memorial Laboratories in Philadelphia designed by Kahn in the late 1950s, in which the glass towers that house the laboratories are attended by slender brick towers containing the servant spaces. In Kahn's buildings, however, the served spaces are not featureless expanses of flexible floor space but specially designed rooms. He saw 'functions' not merely as practical arrangements but as archetypal social institutions deeply embedded in culture. He thought, for example, that every time a teacher addresses a class he or she re-enacts an ancient ritual which has its own spatial tradition, originating perhaps with the guru and his followers sitting in the shade of a tree. An ill-defined, left-over piece of floor space would scarcely be adequate for such an important activity. The same principle applies to promenading through an exhibition of paintings, gathering around a table to eat a meal, or just sitting alone reading a book. In Kahn's famous Salk Institute laboratories at La Jolla, California, completed in 1966, scientists are provided with separate study rooms grouped in little houses overlooking the main courtyard and the Pacific Ocean beyond. The archetypal activity of solitary study is thus separated from the semi-industrial environment of the laboratories themselves and given its own architectural expression.

There are, then, various alternative approaches to managing the relationship between form and function. But is there perhaps something essentially conservative about the whole concept of building types defined in functional or institutional terms? Architecture is often the servant of the establishment, providing the very mechanisms by which society is shaped and disciplined, but should it allow itself to be defined by that servile role? Should it not enjoy its own creative autonomy? Many progressive architects and architectural theorists have tried to free architecture from its servitude to power and money. Sometimes this struggle has involved the invention of new building types, as if the power relationship between the architect and the institution could be reversed, and society could be persuaded to conform to new patterns of behaviour simply by designing the buildings to accommodate them.

In Russia in the 1920s there was much debate among architects and planners about appropriate forms of housing for the new Communist state. The question was: to what extent should traditional domestic functions – cooking, dining, washing, bathing, entertaining – be made communal? Projects were made, and a few were built, in which individual units provided no more than minimal sleeping, resting and personal storage space, all other functions being provided for in canteens, washhouses and club rooms. This arrangement is not unusual, of course, in housing for students, nurses and itinerant workers, but this was supposed to be a new model for the housing of the masses. The idea was that the centuries old 'institution' of the family house and home would eventually be abolished. In the Narkomfin apartment block in Moscow, designed by Moisei Ginsburg in 1928, each apartment was fitted with a minimal kitchen alcove designed to be removed when the residents completed 'the transition to a superior mode of life' and began to prefer the communal catering available in an adjacent block.[5] Apartment blocks, as a building type, merged with workers' clubs to form 'social condensers' which included recreational and educational facilities

The designer of the Narkomfin apartment block in Moscow thought that the spatial configuration of a building might actually change the way people behave. Kitchens in the apartments were minimal in the hope that residents would eventually make 'the transition to a superior mode of life' and use the communal facilities.

such as gymnasiums, libraries and theatres. Here architects were not simply providing what the authorities required; they saw themselves as active contributors to the building of a new kind of society.

More recently, architectural theorists such as Bernard Tschumi and his followers tried to liberate architecture by thinking about human activities in a different, non-institutional way. Inspired by literature and film, they tried to imagine what would happen if the typical architectural brief or programme were to be replaced by a story or narrative, an account of a sequence of events that might occur over time in and around a building. Films and novels do, after all, often contain architecture. Most stories demand an imagined physical setting – the streets, houses, workplaces and public buildings in which the events take place. This imagining of a physical setting (or the borrowing of one from real life) is not so different from the architect's imagining of a new building. The story could be seen as the equivalent of the architect's brief. But whereas a brief is hampered by prejudices, inherited norms and hidden social control mechanisms, a story is a free imaginative creation.

In the first of a series of projects called *The Manhattan Transcripts*, first published in 1981, Bernard Tschumi develops a system of graphic representation in which the work of architecture, if that is what it is, is described in small square images presented in sets of three. Each set consists of a photograph to represent

Is the relationship between form and function a kind of tyranny? Might it be possible to base architecture not on settled institutions and habits but on the 'narratives' of people's lives? Bernard Tschumi's *Manhattan Transcripts* explores this idea and creates architecture of a kind.

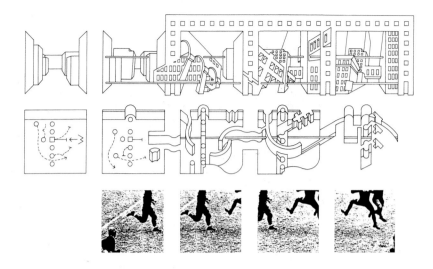

an event, a line drawing to represent the physical setting, and a diagram, like a dance notation, to represent movement. The narrative takes the familiar form of a thriller or detective story. The setting is Central Park in Manhattan. A murderer stalks his victim, the deed is done, the hunt is on, the clues are found, the murderer is apprehended. It is impossible to 'read' this story from the diagrams without an additional explanation, and it is hard to think of this as an architectural project, but it is usefully provocative nevertheless because it makes us see how conventional, institutionalized architecture pigeonholes human life and human imagination.

It can be liberating to misuse a space – to throw a party in a factory or set up a funfair in a market square. In another of Tschumi's *Manhattan Transcripts* projects, five ordinary courtyards in a city block are invaded by strangely incongruous activities like ice-skating, high-wire walking, and the re-enactment of famous battles. The point is not that we should occasionally let our hair down and push the furniture to the walls, but that we are constantly 'misusing' architectural space in our everyday lives. What actually goes on in a building is far too complex and interesting to be captured in a list of officially sanctioned activities. People don't just work in offices, hold meetings in meeting rooms, drink coffee in cafés, and hurry busily along corridors, like actors in some ghastly advertisement. They daydream, plot coups, steal things, run away, engineer encounters, fall in love. Real human activities join together to make the stories of people's lives, and they stubbornly refuse to conform to the labels on the spaces in which they happen. The relationship between function and form, between space and life, is richer than architects normally allow and we too easily lose that richness in our conformity to established procedures such as listing space requirements in briefs and representing designs in plans, sections and elevations.

CHAPTER 5
TRUTH

Le Corbusier famously defined architecture as 'the masterly, correct, and magnificent play of forms in light'. If we are interested in the whole of architecture, not just its visual aspects, then this definition is clearly very limited. This is Le Corbusier the artist speaking – the painter and sculptor – not Le Corbusier the builder or would-be philosopher. Architecture is often lumped together with painting and sculpture for the purposes of critical or historical study, but it is really quite different from those arts and for obvious reasons, such as the fact that it has a practical job to do and will therefore be judged against more than just aesthetic criteria. We saw in the previous chapter how the relationship between space and function, in the sense of human use, has been an important theme in architectural theory. Now it is time to consider the theoretical implications of structure and construction. This aspect of architectural theory is sometimes called 'tectonics' from the Greek word for carpenter or builder.

Of course, even pieces of sculpture have to be constructed and stand up securely, but often the structure that actually bears the loads and stiffens the forms will be concealed or disguised. One thinks, for example of all those equestrian statues in which the horse rears up in a lifelike way, apparently supported only on its hind legs, until we work out that the thick tail that happens to touch the ground is secretly stabilizing the whole form. In the statue, real structure is of secondary importance. Our attention is mainly drawn to the thing represented, not the piece of cast bronze that carries the representation. Architecture can be representational too, as we saw in Chapter 1, but this is not its overt purpose. In an everyday sense it is free form the obligation to represent anything because it has more immediate functions to fulfil. Perhaps this is why its structure demands attention. An architect is forced to decide, for example, whether to show the structure or hide it, whether to make columns and beams visible or embed them in walls

In sculpture, the relationship between structure and appearance is often deceptive. A horse in a statue need not be supported entirely by its legs like a real horse; the bronze tail can make a contribution too. But in architecture, the honest expression of structure has become an orthodoxy.

and ceilings. And as soon as there are decisions like this to be made, theories are bound to emerge about right and wrong ways to make them.

The doctrine of honesty

So should structure be shown or hidden? For much of the twentieth century, among the leaders of architectural opinion, the answer has been 'show it'. Why? Because it is thought to be more 'truthful'. This is not a hard concept to grasp. Obviously to show something is to be open and honest; to hide something might be thought devious and secretive. But are we are thinking about people or buildings? Why should a *building* be honest and truthful? Put this way, the whole concept suddenly seems rather questionable. We might well want to apply moral and ethical standards to the practice of designing and building buildings, just as we would to any social undertaking, but how can words like 'moral' and 'honest' be applied to ordinary practical matters such as the arrangement of beams and columns? It seems unreasonable and yet, over a period of about 150 years, it has gradually become the orthodox view. And this concept of honesty in architecture extends to more than just the showing of structure. It is also applied to the use of materials and the making visible of methods of construction. It was the nineteenth-century art critic, John Ruskin, who gave us the neatest formulation of the concept in his 1849 book *The Seven Lamps of Architecture*. In the chapter 'The Lamp of Truth', he forbids any kind of deceit such as 'the suggestion of a mode of support other than the true one', 'the painting of surfaces to represent some other material', and 'the use of cast or machine made ornaments of any kind'.[1] That last restriction seems rather strange to us. We live in world where almost everything is made in a factory, including

Nineteenth-century architects like A. W. N. Pugin (on the left is his design for St Augustine, Ramsgate, 1846–51) revived Gothic architecture because they thought its informal, asymmetrical planning was an honest answer to the everyday practicalities of human use. Gothic structure was honest too, not hidden away but put on show (below is a cross section of Notre-Dame, Paris).

large parts of buildings, and the idea of machine-made ornament seems relatively inoffensive but in Ruskin's time the centuries old craft of stone carving was only just beginning to be supplanted by the mass production of ornamental pieces in cast iron.

Ruskin loved the medieval architecture that we call Gothic, and tirelessly promoted its revival as the best style for the public buildings of his day. He liked Gothic because it was honest. The informal, asymmetrical plans of churches, abbeys and colleges were honest because they openly revealed the functional relationships between spaces. Why shouldn't the porch of a parish church be off-centre if that was most convenient place to put it? Gothic structure was honest because if you want to know how a Gothic cathedral stands up, all you have to do is look up and see the webs of the vault resting on the ribs and the ribs resting on the piers. Outside you will see, unconcealed, the buttresses that complete the system. The materials and method of construction are honest too: all hand-carved stone, with nothing faked and nothing machine-made.

Well, this supposed honesty of Gothic architecture is not quite as straightforward as it seems at first. How honest is it, for example, to carve the stone capital of a column into a likeness of a wreath of leaves? They are not real leaves. They don't grow or die away. They are artificial or fake leaves designed to give the illusion of life. But for Ruskin this kind of dishonesty is allowable because nobody is really fooled (as one sometimes can be by artificial foliage in modern buildings such as exhibition halls and the atriums of shopping centres). He makes other exceptions. Gilding, for example, which is surely the dressing up of one material to look like another, is allowed in architecture on the grounds that no one would mistake gilded wood or stone for solid gold, whereas in jewellery it is 'altogether to be reprehended' because in that setting someone might indeed mistake it for the real thing. But these are relatively unimportant details. Surely the real objection to the idea that nineteenth-century Gothic architecture is honest is that the whole enterprise is fake – the imitation of a much older style. We have to go back about another 500 years to find the genuine version. An architecture that grew naturally from the material and cultural conditions of medieval England has been artificially revived to serve a very different society with very different technological capabilities. There is something profoundly illogical about this. One can revive everything about a style except its most important quality – its originality.

Twentieth-century Modernists noted this absurdity and set about trying to re-establish an organic relationship between society and its architecture. Instead of imitating old styles, they would attune themselves to the spirit of the machine age and invent new solutions to the social and technical problems of the day. Invention and novelty would take over from tradition and imitation. Ruskin and the Gothicists had held out against mechanized industry, retreating into a medieval fantasy in which buildings were beautiful because the men that built them were happy in their work. The Modernists did the opposite: they embraced industry and tried to make an architecture out of its products. The new architecture would be the honest expression of the new society. The lamp of truth burned even more brightly but the insistence on honesty became less subtle, less forgiving, more dogmatic.

The High Tech style

The twentieth-century version of the doctrine of honesty can be seen very clearly in the style know as High Tech which flourished in Britain in the 1980s.[2] Architects like Norman Foster, Richard Rogers and Nicholas Grimshaw thought of their buildings as assemblages of lightweight factory-made components – 'kits of parts' – rather than as

heavy, solid structures built on firm foundations from the bottom up. And not only were the buildings kits of parts but they looked like kits of parts. The nature of their construction was 'honestly' expressed in their architecture. There was already a long tradition in Modernism of comparing buildings to machines. Le Corbusier, for example, in his enormously influential *Towards a New Architecture*, had juxtaposed pictures of buildings with pictures of ships, aeroplanes and cars. The house was a machine for living in, he said. But this was mainly a conceptual, rather than a visual comparison. If Le Corbusier's Purist villas, such as the Villa Savoye, looked a little like ocean liners well this is not so surprising since one might argue that the superstructure of an ocean liner is already a building. It just happens to be supported on a floating hull. Le Corbusier's buildings did not look much like aeroplanes or cars or other kinds of machine.

High Tech buildings, however, did look like machines. They were made of synthetic materials like metal and glass rather than natural materials like stone and wood, and they took every opportunity to expose their shiny, articulated steel structures, often painted a bright colour. Actual functioning machinery, such as boilers and chillers, with all their attendant tanks, pipes and ducts, were not hidden away as they usually are, but were put boldly on display, often on the outside of the building. This machinery was essential to the functioning of the building and the doctrine of honesty demanded that it be visible.

The Inmos Factory by Richard Rogers, near Newport in Wales, is typical of the style. Its exposed steel trusses are assisted in their unusually long span by a central row of suspension structures towering over the roof. The air conditioning plant sits between these structures, visibly feeding ducts in the roofs on either side. The whole thing, especially in cross section, is indeed vaguely reminiscent of some early experimental aeroplane. It looks as though it has been designed to do a practical job as efficiently as possible with none of the pomp and ceremony associated with traditional architecture. Architecture it is, nevertheless, not engineering, and its apparent purposefulness is as contrived and artificial as any neo-classical facade. There are many cheaper, more practical ways to do the job that this building does.

High Tech buildings really do look like machines (shown here: the Inmos Factory by Richard Rogers). In this style, the doctrine of honesty was taken to extremes. Structure had to be clearly visible, preferably on the outside, and every column, strut and tension rod had to have a real structural function. It was still architecture, though, not just engineering.

Nevertheless, if we can accept this proviso, the building's most important characteristic is its complete, almost puritanical honesty. All of this visible structure is real. It does a real job and it is seen to do a real job. It is made of steel and nobody could possibly mistake it for any other material. Those air handlers really handle air, pushing it down those real ducts, and that square gridded, lightweight panelled, non-load-bearing external wall is exactly that.

The High Tech architects never talked much about Ruskin, but they were strict, unquestioning followers of his religion of truth nevertheless. Even when, later, they got bored with steel and glass and began to rediscover more traditional materials, they stuck to their principles. Michael Hopkins, an important figure in the early development of the High Tech style, completely abandoned the machine aesthetic in the later phase of his career, developing a taste for brick walls and wood-framed roofs covered with lead. But his brickwork, such as that

Michael Hopkins began his career in the High Tech camp but his later buildings, such as Glyndebourne Opera House, used traditional materials such as brick, timber and lead. The doctrine of honesty, however, was if anything even more strictly maintained.

of his Glyndebourne opera house of 1994, is always real, load-bearing brickwork, with real piers and real arches, never merely a comfortingly traditional curtain to conceal a steel or concrete frame.

High Tech is an extreme example of the doctrine of architectural honesty. Most modern buildings adopt a more pragmatic approach, allowing a certain degree of concealment and deception where it might simplify the details or make the structure more economical. So timber framed walls are cement-rendered, creating the impression that they are made of solid masonry, steel frames are covered over by panelled walls and ceilings, and pipes and ducts are concealed in service cores so that their designers don't have to worry too much about what they look like. Nevertheless there are, among architects, certain limits to this licence, certain taboos. For example, in British popular housing it is common for commercial developers, who mostly ignore architectural theory, to build a brick wall around a timber framed house for the very good reason that house-buyers prefer the solid, traditional look of brickwork. Architects however, who are not much involved in popular housing, object to this, not because the buyer is actually being deceived but on the grounds that it is dishonest in the Ruskinian sense. A timber frame house, they will argue, has no right to pretend to be a brick house and should be clad in some kind of light cladding, such as weatherboarding or tile hanging, which clearly indicates its true nature.

The classical tradition

As we have seen, the doctrine of honesty has its origins in the nineteenth-century Gothic revival. But what about classical architecture? Most of the history of western architecture is the history of the great architectural tradition inaugurated by the Greek temple. Historians give it different names – Hellenistic, Roman, Renaissance, Mannerist, Baroque, Greek Revival and so on – as it progresses down the centuries but all are versions of the classical. And none of them pays much heed to the Ruskinian doctrine of honesty. How could they when the original ancient prototype was itself 'dishonest'? The Greek temple is basically a

representation in stone of an even older wooden original. So in a sense
it is a fake. As that other great nineteenth-century Gothic revivalist and
anti-classicist, A. W. N. Pugin put it:

> 'Grecian architecture is essentially wooden in its construction…
> and is it not extraordinary that when the Greeks commenced
> building in stone, the properties of this material did not suggest
> to them some different and improved mode of construction?'[3]

Extraordinary perhaps only when viewed through rationalizing
nineteenth-century eyes. In fact, theorists of the seventeenth and
eighteenth centuries had already begun to question the irrational
nature of classical architecture. Marc-Antoine Laugier, for example,
in his *Essai sur l'Architecture*, first published in 1753, argued that
classical architecture had developed over the centuries through a
process of imitation and refinement from an original, primitive hut.[4]
The frontispiece of his pamphlet shows the female personification of
architecture pointing at just such a hut with a double-pitched, leaf-
covered roof (pediment) supported by horizontal branches (entablature)
resting on vertical tree trunks still rooted in the ground (columns). These
three, according to Laugier, were the primary elements of architecture.
All other elements – walls, windows and doors, for example – were
secondary. In Laugiers' view, the parts of a building that bear load
were more important than the parts of a building that divide space.
As a result of this kind of thinking, architects began to reject common
ornamental features of classical architecture such as attached columns
or pilasters, pediments or gables used where there was no actual roof to
terminate, and superimposed orders used externally where there was no
corresponding division of levels inside the building. We can see the effect

of Laugier's rationalism in a building like the church of Sainte-Geneviève in Paris (now the Pantheon), designed in the 1760s by Jacques-Germain Soufflot, with its proper temple portico, its mostly plain external walls and its free-standing internal columns.

Ornament and pattern-making

But there was, and is, another way of looking at the question of honesty in architecture, and to examine this alternative view we must turn to another nineteenth-century theorist: Gottfried Semper. Semper's influence on the architecture of the twentieth century was minimal but in recent years, as the Modernist spell has weakened, interest in his theories has revived. Semper was a German architect who designed several important buildings such as the opera house in Dresden and the polytechnic school (ETH) in Zurich. He was no Gothic revivalist but a firm believer in the continued rightness and relevance of the classical tradition. His major theoretical work, only recently translated into English, is *Der Stil in den technischen und tektonischen Künsten oder Praktische Ästhetik*, a long, unfinished, difficult and often ambiguous text which attempts to capture the essence of style not just in architecture but in all 'technical and tectonic arts'. More concise and approachable is his earlier essay, *The Four Elements of Architecture*, published in 1851. In it he sets out a strikingly original account of the genesis of the art of architecture. Like Laugier, Semper imagines the source of architecture to be a primitive hut, but his version is different in important ways. The four elements mentioned in the title are: the hearth, the mound or foundation, the roof and the enclosure. At first this seems similar to Laugier's system but whereas Laugier identifies the roof and the permanent structure that supports it as the main carrier of architectural meaning, Semper allows each of his four elements to find its own level of importance according to circumstances.

> 'According to how different human societies developed under the varied influences of climate, natural surroundings, social relations and racial dispositions, the combinations in which the four elements of architecture were arranged also had to change, with some elements becoming more developed while others receded into the background.'[5]

Thus the fixed, hierarchical nature of architecture as envisaged by Laugier is subverted. But Semper goes further. He sees the elements not primarily as functioning parts of a building but as representatives of different ways of making things. The hearth represents ceramics (and possibly metalwork), the mound represents masonry, the roof represents carpentry and the wall represents weaving. Why weaving? Because, according to Semper, the first space-dividing elements were free-standing hurdles made from woven twigs. These later developed into carpets and tapestries, which were hung from the carpentered frames of houses to separate the rooms. This emphasis on weaving is the most original aspect of Semper's theory and it has profound consequences for the way building is thought about and described. For Laugier, the non-load-bearing wall is a secondary element; for Semper it is primary.

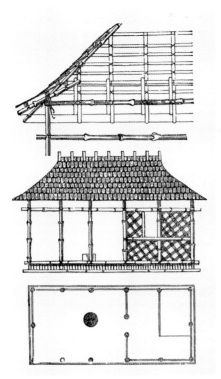

Citing an ancient Assyrian example (then recently discovered), he
argues that the alabaster bas-reliefs carved in the walls of Nineveh
(fine examples can be seen in the British Museum) are really petrified
versions of ornamental carpets. Carpets may have been hung on stone
walls, but it was the carpets that were the original space dividers, not the
walls. Eventually, carpet and wall were combined in the bas-reliefs and
the ornamental became confused with the functional. The ornamental
took precedence, however, because Semper saw the very act of weaving
as the expression of an innate ordering or pattern-making impulse
in humankind. After he had written the *Four Elements*, Semper came
across a convenient confirmation of his ethnographic speculations in
a Trinidadian hut displayed in the Great Exhibition of 1851 in London.
Drawings of this hut, with its bamboo frame and textile walls, have
served ever since as the standard illustration of his theories.

In his later work, *Der Stil*, Semper develops these theories in their
full philosophical depth. The pattern-making that is the essence of
architecture takes on special importance as a 'cosmogonic' or world-
creating activity. Architecture is more akin to other rhythmic cosmogonic
arts such as music and dance than to the visual arts of painting or
sculpture. The idea of the mask, of the altering of appearances, is also
identified as a primary characteristic of architecture. Architecture is
dressing. It is the clothes, the adornment of the body, not the body itself.
The world-creating function of architecture depends on pretence, in
the same way that the illusory effect of a figurative painting depends
on the ignoring of the actual material substance of the paint and the
canvas. Concepts like truth to materials and the honest expression of
structure are foreign to Semper's way of thinking. If a form developed in

one material (carved in wood, say) is reproduced in another (cast in iron, perhaps) then this is only the necessary fiction that architecture has always dealt in. Far from being a moral lapse, it is the very essence of the craft.

An important aspect of Semper's theory is that it 'dislocates' the activity of building. Parts of buildings, like ceramic hearths or woven walls, are the products of crafts or industries that are independent of, and prior to building. Elements may be made in locations remote from the site and when they are brought together for assembly they are combined not according to some fixed system or 'correct' hierarchy but in configurations that change according to circumstances. For example, in ancient Greek architecture the dominant element is the 'tectonic' or carpentered frame, which develops into the Doric, Ionic and Corinthian orders. But in ancient Roman architecture, the 'stereotomic' masonry mound becomes dominant, rising from the earth in arches, vaults and domes. What happens on the site is less important, less essential, than the prior developments in what Semper called the industrial arts. The primary human act of world-making is not the construction of a primitive hut but the weaving of a carpet or, ultimately, the tying of a single ornamental knot. Ideas like truth to materials and the honest expression of structure become irrelevant because in Semper's system the normal priority of structure over ornament is reversed.

So, for Semper, architecture is the making of an artificial world. Its artificiality is its essence. It does not aspire to be 'real' or 'natural' or 'true'. Like every other art it is a kind of fiction, an attempt to understand the world by imitating it. When we watch a play in the theatre we willingly suspend our disbelief. We know that it is art, not reality. But it may well teach us something about reality and about our relationship to it. Architecture is the same. Its origin lies not in the building of the first practical shelter but in the pattern-making that is humankind's first attempt to come to terms with the world. We make patterns in sound and call it music, we make patterns in space with our bodies and call it dance, and we make patterns with form and line and colour and call it ornament. This is not some inessential, later embellishment of a more fundamental structure. It is there from the start. It is the original motive of architecture.

In orthodox Modernist thinking, ornament is unnecessary, part of the useless baggage of the nineteenth century. Modernists think that architecture should consist of real things – real structure, real materials, real solutions to real problems. Ornament distracts from this reality, covers it up, denies it, fictionalizes it. But from the alternative, Semperian point of view, ornament is conceptually prior to problem solving. Humankind perceives certain rhythms or patterns in the world – day and night, sun and rain, light and shade – and conceives the possibility that they might be imitated in art. Without this original impulse to 'imitate nature or complete what nature cannot finish', to quote Aristotle, the idea of constructing, say, a primitive hut would never have arisen.

Ornament and imitation are inseparable. Most ornament is imitative and often what it imitates is natural, organic form, whether vegetable or animal. The Art Nouveau style that flourished under different names (Liberty in Britain, Jugendstil in Germany, Modernisme

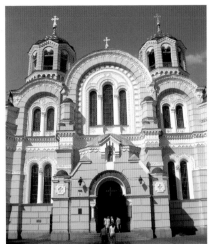

in Catalonia) at the beginning of the last century was an attempt to sweep away the stylistic confusion of the nineteenth century and replace it with a 'modern' style that reconnected ornament with its original inspiration – nature. The iron railings and canopies of Hector Guimard's Paris Metro entrances, for example, curve and twist and seem to grow, sometimes like bones, sometimes like the stems and tendrils of plants. Glass canopies look like the translucent leaves of tropical trees, and lamp standards droop and nod like exotic flowers. But of course animal and vegetable forms had been a part of architectural ornament for centuries. To what extent the volutes of an Ionic capital were inspired by the spiral forms of rams horns is uncertain but the acanthus leaves that wrap the Corinthian capital are straightforwardly figurative. Most architectural ornament is either naturalistic or abstracted from natural forms. (An important exception is the calligraphic ornament of Islamic architecture, which arose because of the Qur'an's discouragement of figurative art in general.) So what exactly were the Art Nouveau architects sweeping away? They seemed to take the imitative aspect of ornament for granted; what they did not do is imitate other styles of architecture.

Representational ornament

In Chapter 1 we looked at the many ways in which architecture could be said to be 'representational'. One of them was the representation of one building by another. This kind of representation was the theoretical foundation of the various nineteenth-century stylistic revivals. So, St Vladimir's Cathedral in Kiev, for example, is in some sense a representation of an ancient Byzantine church. Thinking about this in the context of ornament, we realize that the ornamentation of

The Palazzo Rucellai in Florence has an imaginary building drawn on its facade. The imaginary building is held up by columns and beams, not solid walls like the real building. But is it imaginary? Is it perhaps an idealized Colosseum?

It was the Colosseum that set the rules for the correct arrangement of columns and beams. But this is curious because the Colosseum is not a framed building. Its real structure is made of masonry and concrete formed into massive arches and vaults. The framed structure is merely ornament – and this is the basis of all Classical architecture.

The tower of St George's
Church, Bloomsbury,
is a stack of miniature
buildings, including
a triumphal arch, a
Palladian villa and
the tomb of Mausolus,
crowned by a statue
of King George I. This
not a 'design' in the
modern sense.

buildings often consists of representations of architectural elements
such as columns, beams and arches. Look, for example, at the facade of
Alberti's Palazzo Rucellai in Florence. Apart from the cornice at the top,
its various features project only slightly from the main wall plane. It is
so flat that, seen straight on, it almost looks like a drawing. Or perhaps it
is two drawings, one overlaid on the other. First comes the basic carcass
of the building: a three-storey block with windows spaced at regular
intervals. Overlaid on this is drawing number one which represents an
arcuated and rusticated structure, with deep grooves cut between the
stones and arches over every window. Then overlaid on this is a second
drawing representing a completely different kind of building, still three
storeys, but this time a trabeated structure of beams and columns. And
perhaps the whole thing is a copy, or at least a version, of a specific
ancient Roman building – the Colosseum in Rome, which combines
arcuated and trabeated forms in a similar way.

Classical architecture – the tradition to which Gottfried Semper
was committed in his own practice – could almost be defined as the
re-composition of features borrowed from other buildings. Sometimes

The aedicule or little shrine is a basic component of traditional architectural ornament. The windows of the Palazzo Farnese in Rome (above left) are all aedicules. The facade looks like a three-storey street of little classical temples.

Aedicules appear in Gothic buildings too. What is the south porch of Chartres Cathedral (above right) if not a collection of little buildings, each a complete piece of architecture in its own right? Some stand on the ground, some are raised up on the shoulders of their neighbours.

Hindu temples (left) are also aedicular. The smallest component buildings are mere niches for sculpture, but the accumulative effect is of burgeoning abundance, symbolizing the creative power of the universe.

the borrowings are actual quotations from specific buildings, sometimes they are taken from the store of traditional features common to many buildings. Look, for example, at the tower of Nicholas Hawksmoor's St George's Church, Bloomsbury, London. It is a vertical stack of borrowed buildings. Square on plan, the main shaft of the tower rises to a height well above the big Corinthian portico. Already the church looks like two buildings because about two thirds of the way up a prominent projecting horizontal band or string course seems to indicate a new ground level and a fresh start. Above the band the shaft is terminated by a kind of two-way triumphal arch, complete with projecting cornice as if to indicate that we have reached the top. But not at all. Standing on top of the triumphal arch is a complete miniature temple, with an Ionic portico on each of its four sides, like Palladio's Villa Rotonda. On top of the little temple is yet another complete piece of architecture, a spire in the form of a stepped pyramid that is a recreation of the ancient tomb of Mausolus (the original mausoleum) at Hallicarnassus, as described by Pliny. Finally, to crown the whole composition, we have not a cross or a weathervane but a statue of King George I. And 'composition' is surely the right word. This is not a 'design' in the modern sense. It is not the result of any systematic analysis of functional requirements. Efficiency and practicality were not high priorities in its creation. We are a long way away from Ruskinian and Modernist ideas about truth and reality. Hawksmoor's tower is practically all ornament. It is dressed up in antique clothes. It is a fiction that relies on imitation. It creates a new world by borrowing buildings from history and mythology. But this, as Semper would say, is what architecture has always done. This is what the word architecture means.

The 'aedicule' or 'little shrine' is a useful concept when considering architectural ornament of the Hawksmoor kind. The temple half-way up the St George's tower is an unusually complete aedicule, a scale model of a whole temple. More often aedicules are partial or fragmentary. The first floor windows of the Palazzo Farnese in Rome, for example, are aedicules, each a representation of a little temple with a pair of columns supporting an entablature and a pediment. This is a very common motif in Classical architecture but aedicules are even more common in the Gothic tradition. John Summerson wrote a famous essay, 'Heavenly Mansions', in which he argued that Gothic cathedrals should be interpreted as agglomerations of aedicules, of buildings within buildings.[6] The south porch of Chartres Cathedral, for example, is divided into three aedicules, each with its own gable roof and these in turn contain smaller aedicules in the form of canopied niches for statues. At high level between the gables the statues are housed in two single-storey, three-bay vaulted structures, each a complete piece of architecture in its own right. We find aedicules too in other architectural traditions, notably in Hindu temples, in which small aedicules are piled up to form artificial mountains of teeming mythical sculpture.

Structure and ornament

Is there any sense in which Semper's vision of architecture is still relevant today? Have imitation, ornament, dressing up and world-making vanished completely from architecture? Perhaps they are still present

in a latent or hidden form. We saw how, for example, even the Inmos Factory (see page 87) is more than just a piece of practical engineering. High Tech buildings might look a little like bridges or oil refineries or aeroplanes but in essence they are quite different. Exposing mechanical services on the outside of a building is not actually a very practical thing to do. It is done not to make the building more efficient but to create an image of efficiency, an image that places the building in that sphere of culture called 'modern technology' so it can benefit from the prestige of that association. Is that image not a kind of fiction, a kind of artificial world? And what about the exposed steel structure, so beautifully articulated, with its compression and tension members clearly distinguished from one another? Is there not a hint of ornament about it? It is, in a sense, completely honest. It does a real structural job of work. But it certainly isn't the most efficient or practical of all the possible structural solutions. It was selected not for engineering reasons but for architectural reasons – because it was thought pleasing to the eye. It surely stands in the long tradition of using structural elements as ornaments.

We can look at a lot of modern architecture the same way. Ornament and imitation have not disappeared, they have merely been suppressed and disguised. Architects often talk about 'good detailing'. Good construction detailing is important for practical reasons – to ensure water-tightness, or durability or structural integrity. But that isn't what the architects mean. They mean a certain neat simplicity or elegance in the detail and often this will involve some concealment or deception. A famous example from the Modernist canon is the external mullion detail of the Seagram Building in New York by Mies van der Rohe. It is a steel-framed building clad in a curtain wall of glass and bronze. Ruskinian honesty would seem to demand that the steel frame be visible. But it can't be because the steel frames of skyscrapers have to be fire-proofed. So Mies, wishing to preserve at least the quality and feel of a metal-framed building, attached vertical bronze mullions to the facade at regular intervals. They have no practical function. They are purely ornamental.

Modern architecture is ornamented too, but in more restrained ways. The curtain walls of Mies van der Rohe's Seagram Building in New York (1954–58; above left) are graced by bronze columns or mullions which are structurally completely redundant but which emphasize the handsome proportions of the building like the seams and creases of a smart business suit.

Mies van der Rohe again, this time his little house for Edith Farnsworth in Illinois (1945–51; above right). Is this building ornamented in any way? Perhaps not, but there is no doubt that it is classical in spirit. Mies was educated in the tradition of the great German Neoclassicist, Karl Friedrich Schinkel.

The Museum of Modern Literature in Marbach am Neckar, by David Chipperfield, completed in 2006, is stripped down and rather austere, but no one can look at its colonnades without thinking of Greek or Roman temples. They are ornamental in the broadest sense.

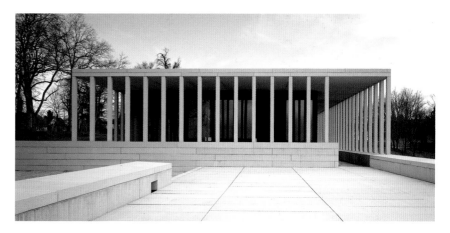

Herzog and de Meuron's library at Eberswalde is a somewhat literal-minded attempt to revive ornament in modern architecture. The photographs etched onto the concrete panels are linear and repetitive, like the triglyphs and metopes of Doric entablature, but their relation to the building as a whole is arbitrary.

Note that, as architectural ornament, the Seagram mullions are completely traditional. Like the pilasters of the Pallazzo Rucellai, they are imitations of structural members, in this case steel columns. Mies was educated in the nineteenth-century Neoclassical tradition of which Karl Friedrich Schinkel was the great hero. The buildings of Mies's maturity, such as the Farnsworth House or Crown Hall on the Illinois Institute of Technology campus, are clearly not ornamented in the usual sense of the word, but they are nevertheless Classical in spirit and to that extent can be said to be traditionally imitative. And the Classical tradition is still very much alive in the twenty-first century. David Chipperfield's Museum of Modern Literature at Marbach am Neckar in Germany, for example, is crowned by what is unmistakably a Classical temple complete with full peristyle. There are no volutes or acanthuses on display but this is undoubtedly an ornamental building.

The curtain-like concrete facades of Caruso St John's Nottingham Contemporary art gallery (2009) are ornamented by floral patterns borrowed from lace-making, a local industry. So in this ornament there are two layers of representation: of the lace, and of the flowers.

In these Classical modern buildings ornament is latent or suppressed but there has also in recent years been a revival of interest in frankly figurative ornament, often derived from the function of the building. Herzog and de Meuron's technical school library at Eberswalde in Germany, for example, is completely covered externally by old photographs etched onto the glass and concrete panels. Like the triglyphs and metopes of a Doric entablature, the photographs are repeated in horizontal bands, with one photograph per panel. Ornament and construction are therefore to some extent integrated but there is almost no three-dimensional modelling and the overall impression is of a concrete monolith only slightly enlivened by the busy pattern of the pictures. The outline of Caruso St John's Nottingham Contemporary art gallery is more complicated because it has to fit itself into an awkward split-level site, but the overall effect of its fluted pre-cast concrete and gold-anodized aluminium external walls is of curtains drawn round the site boundary rather than of articulated three-dimensional form. The curtain analogy is appropriate because the gallery is in what used to be the lace-making part of town and the concrete panels are etched with a pattern derived from an actual sample of Victorian lace. There is, therefore, a double imitation here – the concrete pattern imitates the lace, which in turn depicts a floral motif. As with the Herzog and de Meuron building, ornament and construction are to some extent integrated, but the effect is to undermine rather than reinforce the constructed, tectonic aspect of the building. Perhaps this should be called decoration rather than ornament.

These recent revivals of ornament seem to have forgotten the possibility that ornament's subject matter might be found in the tectonic forms of architecture itself. Modernism's insistence on invention and novelty has outlawed the imitation on which ornament is based. But perhaps the problem is deeper than that. In an important book called *Studies in Tectonic Culture*, Kenneth Frampton argues that tectonic culture is becoming irrelevant in a world of spectacle and simulation. In their education and practice, architects are more and more distanced from the realities of construction, and computers, which have revolutionized architectural practice, seem only to increase the distance. The typical products of large, fully computer-based practices, have a strangely arbitrary quality, as if there were no difference between a computer model, which floats in a digital void, and a real building, which needs a real structure to hold it up. Sometimes the effect can be exhilarating, like the flame-like forms of Frank Gehry's Guggenheim Museum in Bilbao, but more often they look awkward and wilful like the scale-less, boxy loop of OMA's Central China TV building in Beijing, which reveals almost nothing of its constructed nature.

To the orthodox, Modernist way of thinking, Semper's and Ruskin's theories are incompatible. There seems to be an opposition between ornament, which is essentially imitative, and the doctrine of tectonic honesty, which seems to forbid imitation. And yet Ruskin saw no such opposition. In his *Lectures on Architecture*, he declares straightforwardly that 'ornamentation is the principal part of architecture'. 'The great law is,' he says, 'convenience first, and then the noblest decoration possible.'[7] For him, the important distinction is between architecture and mere building, and it is ornament that marks that distinction. Perhaps it still does. Tectonics often provides the subject matter of ornament. The two principles are allied, not opposed, and in a digital culture that favours image over substance, both are under threat.

The ornamentation of OMA's Central China TV building in Beijing (2010) bears little relation to the form or structure of the building. The idea that tectonics might provide the imagery of ornament has been rejected – or forgotten.

CHAPTER 6
NATURE

What does 'organic architecture' mean? In casual conversation and in coffee-table books it often simply means buildings or parts of buildings that bear some superficial resemblance to animals or plants. We normally expect architecture to be regular and rectilinear and when it isn't, when, for example, it includes curved forms other than simple arches, we call it 'organic'. The entrance hall and staircase of Victor Horta's Hotel Tassel in Brussels – a fine example of the late nineteenth-century style known as Art Nouveau – might be said to be organic in this sense. Iron columns and balustrades curve and twist like the stems and tendrils of a climbing plant. There is no practical or functional justification for these 'whiplash' forms. They are mainly decorative, like their painted counterparts on the plastered walls that enclose the space.

 Are there other ways in which a building may be described as organic? Do the materials used to build it have any bearing on the matter? A building made from vegetable or animal materials like wood or reeds or woven wool must, in a literal sense, be more organic that one made of mineral substances like stone or concrete or steel. But it seems that, conceptually, it doesn't really work that way. The average suburban American house is mainly built of wood but, dressed up as it is in one of the common 'reminiscent' styles, it certainly wouldn't be described as organic. And if a house in the forest with a structure made from the unprocessed limbs of trees and a roof covered in moss and grass is called organic, it is more for its general spirit of closeness to nature than for the materials used in its construction. On the other hand, there are plenty of examples of 'organic' reinforced concrete buildings, if only because concrete is a fluid material that lends itself to curving, animal-like forms, whether muscular or membranous. The nested concrete sails or shells (note the organic metaphor) of Jørn Utzon's Sydney Opera House are a case in point. So we are back with simple, physical resemblance as the main criterion.

The Art Nouveau
decoration of Victor
Horta's Hotel Tassel
in Brussels borrows
forms from nature,
but is this enough to
make it an 'organic'
building? In architecture,
'organic' usually means
something deeper, more
a matter of structure
and process than of
superficial resemblance.

But of course the concept of organic architecture is more
complicated than that. Perhaps the most famous organic architect
was Frank Lloyd Wright. There are a couple of notable exceptions
like the Guggenheim Museum in New York with its expanding spiral
ramp (a snail shell?), and the cantilevered terraces of Fallingwater (a
bracken fungus?), but Wright's buildings did not usually resemble living
organisms. They were organic in a deeper sense, a sense that he himself
was largely responsible for establishing in the architectural theory of
the twentieth century. For Wright, a building was organic if it emerged
naturally from the circumstances of its creation: the landscape, the
climate, the site, the functions it had to serve, the society it supported,
and the free, creative imagination of its architect. Unity of space and
form was important, not in the sense that the buildings were simple
or monolithic but in the sense that different parts were related to
one another according to a unified concept, like the limbs and organs
of an animal. In the introduction to the *Wasmuth Portfolio*, a lavish
monograph of his work published in Germany in 1910, Wright wrote this:

> 'But underneath forms in all ages were certain conditions which
> determined them. In them all was a human spirit in accord with
> which they came to be; and where the forms were true forms, they
> will be found to be organic forms – an outgrowth, in other words,
> of conditions of life and work they arose to express.'[1]

He goes on to write about Renaissance and Gothic architecture, making
it very clear which he preferred: Gothic. This may seem surprising given
that the buildings illustrated in the portfolio, the so-called Prairie Style

Reinforced concrete is an inorganic material but it is cast and therefore lends itself to curved and flowing forms, which remind us of natural organisms. The Sydney Opera House (1956–73; left) has been compared to a plate of oyster shells. Frank Lloyd Wright declared himself to be an organic architect and yet his buildings, like the Robie House (1908; centre left), are strictly rectilinear compositions.

Bruce Goff's Bavinger House in Oklahoma (1950–55; left) seems more convincingly organic, like something that has grown in the forest and which welcomes wild plant life into its interior, but many of the materials it uses, such as glass and steel, are synthetic.

houses such as the Robie House in Chicago, seemed the very opposite of Gothic: not soaring, vertical structures but low, wide, ground-hugging compositions with big roof overhangs. But Wright had been influenced by the great French theorist Viollet-le-Duc, who found in Gothic architecture the perfect organic expression of the structural potential of stone. It was not the Gothic forms themselves that Wright admired, but the way that they seemed to be 'in accord' with the nature of the material and the 'human spirit' of the time. Renaissance architecture, in contrast, was an 'inglorious masquerade devoid of vital significance or true spiritual value'.

Form, material, space

The Gothic tradition, whether in its original medieval form or as revived in the nineteenth century, provides a good illustration of certain aspects of the organic analogy in architecture. Standing in a High Gothic building like Bourges Cathedral is a little like standing in a forest. The piers of the nave arcade are remarkably like tree trunks from which the arches and vault ribs grow like branches. Was this resemblance apparent to the medieval masons? Was it a deliberate effect? Is the building a representation of a forest? Probably not, or at least not in the simple sense that a theatre set might represent a forest. If the masons and their

Gothic and organic seem to go together. It isn't merely that being in the thirteenth-century nave of Bourges Cathedral is a little like being in the forest. The whole structural and material logic of the building seems organic, like the processes of nature. The builders of Bourges Cathedral knew little about those processes in the scientific sense, but perhaps their daily contact with the forces of nature invested them with an organic instinct.

The wooden columns and simple clay-tiled roof of this garden pavilion might encourage us to call it organic. But it is also classical, taking its formal rules from history, not nature, and asserting its artificiality as a contrast to the growing forms around it.

Palladio's Villa Rotonda (1570) is an example of what Frank Lloyd Wright called the 'inglorious masquerade' of Renaissance architecture. One might argue that its four porticos seem to reach out to the landscape, inviting nature to enter, but inside the space is controlled by a rigid geometry. Form derived from history is imposed upon matter in a deliberately artificial way.

clients thought of their cathedral as a representation of anything at all it was the Kingdom of Heaven as described in the Bible, and this only in a rather abstract way. So if the cathedral is 'organic' it is not a question of simple resemblance. Rather it is organic because its form arises 'naturally' from the conjunction of a human idea with the capacities and limitations of stone as a building material. That human idea is hard to define but quite obviously it involves a preference for height and verticality of proportion, and a striving for a certain spatial effect, a diffusion of light through an interior that is complex and articulated but at the same time unified. These qualities symbolize a religious idea, a reaching up to heaven and a celebration of divine radiance.

We usually think of stone as a massive, heavy material, but in a Gothic cathedral it becomes slender and light, as if magically transformed, by some process that would be the opposite of petrifaction, into a linear, fibrous material like wood. In order to persuade stone to adopt this character it is necessary to devise all sorts of clever structural details like pointed arches, ribbed vaults and flying buttresses. In a modern, reinforced concrete structure slenderness is easily achieved because tensile forces are resisted by the steel rods buried in the concrete. But the medieval cathedral is simply a pile of stones, one resting on another with nothing but a thin layer of mortar to join them. Every weight has to be balanced by a counter weight, every arch held in place either by a buttress or by another arch. The characteristic forms of Gothic architecture therefore arise partly for symbolic reasons and partly because they are essential to the stability of the structure. Form and material are related to one another functionally, as they are in a natural organism, and the motive for the progressive refinement of this relationship is a religious idea or, in Frank Lloyd Wright's terms, 'a human spirit'.

So how does the 'inglorious masquerade' of Renaissance architecture fit into the picture? In this context it serves mainly to represent the opposite of the organic. To put it at its simplest: in a Gothic building form grows out of matter; in a Renaissance building, form is imposed upon matter. The forms of Renaissance architecture were provided not by nature, or by anything akin to a natural process, but by history, by the classical tradition stretching back to ancient Greece and Rome. When an architect adorns his or her building with a classical 'order' it matters little what the columns and entablatures are made of. Often they will be made of stone, but wood or plastered brick are perfectly acceptable alternatives. It will still be a classical building. A loose relationship between form and material is tolerated.

But the relationship between form and material is only one aspect of the argument. Wright's version of the organic analogy also has a spatial dimension. In a Renaissance building like Palladio's Villa Rotonda, space is controlled by a rigid, static geometry of bilateral symmetries and harmonic proportions. This is a collection of rooms, each one a coherent, separate space, like a little world of its own. Together the rooms form a geometrical and hierarchical pattern, clearly visible in the plan, but the actual experience of the building's interior is episodic, a string of separate spaces rather than a unified whole. Contrast this with the interior of Frank Lloyd Wright's Robie House (see page 108) which consists not of separate rooms but of spaces that flow into one another – the dining space flowing round and through the combined staircase and fire place into the living space beyond, then on again through the mostly glazed external wall, out onto the terrace under the big roof overhang. So it is not just the interior space that is unified. The flow of space continues out into the surrounding landscape or, in this case, the surrounding streets of a Chicago suburb. The Villa Rotonda also reaches out to the surrounding landscape, almost literally. Four identical flights of steps lead up to four identical porticos as if inviting the whole world to come in and take a look around. But at the same time, the form somehow remains contained and aloof. It wishes to distinguish itself from the woods and fields that surround it, not become part of them. It seems to say: 'I am a man-made object; I am not organic.'

The space inside the Villa Rotonda (see page 106) is contained, divided, static and artificial, but the space inside Wright's Robie House is free, unified, dynamic and (in a sense) natural. It flows through and around the solid parts of the building – through the chimney, for example, through the external walls, out onto the terraces and on into the city. It is more like external than internal space, wild space, rather than domestic space.

So organic architecture has several different aspects. It favours a close relationship between form and materials, allowing form to grow out of material rather than imposing form on material. In a similar way, it seeks spatial solutions not in abstract patterns or traditional configurations but in the practical and spiritual needs of particular social and cultural institutions, from the religious visions of medieval Europe to the secular expansiveness of wealthy industrialists in early twentieth-century Chicago. It also wishes to belong to the landscape that surrounds it, including the climate that made that landscape. It wants to join in with nature, not remain aloof from it. It might, incidentally, bear some physical resemblance to something organic like a tree or a forest, and it might literally be made of organic materials, but neither of these characteristics is essential to the concept. Most fundamentally, perhaps, organic architecture looks to nature rather than history for its inspiration – not just what nature looks like, but the way nature works. Renaissance architects took traditional forms and imposed them on nature and society. The organic analogy put things the other way round. Nature and society come first and it is they that give rise to architectural form.

Vernacular architecture

And the architect? Perhaps he or she is not as important as we think. In 1964 Bernard Rudofsky wrote a now famous book called *Architecture without Architects* based on an exhibition at the Museum of Modern Art in New York. It is a selective survey of the 'vernacular' architecture of the world – buildings built in societies that have no concept of architecture as a profession or an academic discipline. Architects, by definition, can't design vernacular buildings. This may seem a rather sweeping statement, but we must remember that the cultural institution we call architecture emerged relatively recently in the west. We even hesitate to call the designers of Gothic cathedrals 'architects'. Rudofsky's idea is not that buildings build themselves or that, in vernacular architecture, there is no one making important decisions such as how big a building should be and what materials should be used in its construction. He simply means that these 'anonymous' builders do not fit the normal western concept of 'architect'. Underneath this observation lies a version of the organic analogy. Some of Rudofsky's examples now seem eminently architectural. For example, to exclude the vaults and domes of fifteenth-century Persian mosques from conventional architectural history now seems culturally blinkered. And to describe the domestic architecture of certain Mediterranean settlements as 'classical vernacular' implies a direct link with mainstream architectural history. But other pictures (*Architecture without Architects* is basically a picture book), like the aerial shots of Zanzibar and Marrakesh, or the extraordinary panoramas of Dogon villages in western Sudan, seem to show something alien to the very idea of design as a deliberate act. They look like organic accretions: forests or coral reefs or insects' nests. A Moroccan courtyard house is certainly a piece of deliberate design, but when we see 500 of them packed together in a woven mat of streets and alleyways we can almost believe that they grew naturally like a population of organisms, each one an individual, but resembling one another like members of a species. And why shouldn't we think of them this way? Human beings are natural organisms, after all, and we are not the only animals that build shelters for ourselves. This is not the place for an extended discussion of animal

An aerial view of houses in Morocco from the book *Architecture without Architects*. This is what is sometimes called 'vernacular' architecture. The word associates architecture with spoken language, the common language of the people. Each of these individual houses was, in a sense, 'designed', but in accordance with a tradition that has grown naturally out of climate, available materials and cultural preferences.

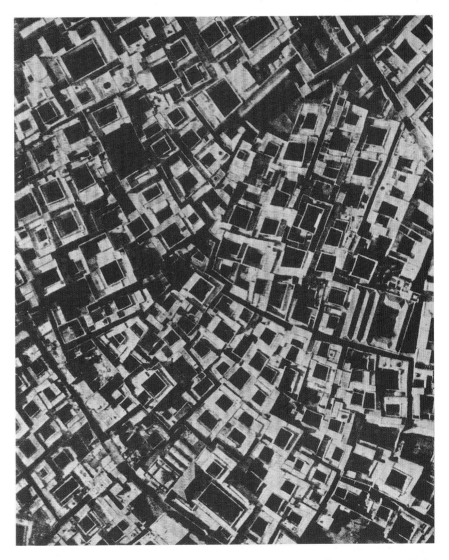

architecture, but think of birds' nests, rabbit warrens, beavers' dams, termite mounds – the list is endless. Is there perhaps a natural way for human beings to build? Well, no. Human society is always cultural, never entirely 'natural' (which is itself a cultural notion). But if we were to place the shelters we build on some kind of scale from the artificial to the natural, from the pre-conceived to the organic, then a lot of vernacular architecture would have to be placed at the organic end of that scale.

Relationships and processes

It should be clear by now that when we are thinking about organic architecture we are not just thinking about finished buildings. The concept of the organic seems to have as much to do with relationships and processes as with appearances. The way a building works might be described as organic even if its form is as rigid and pre-conceived as that of a Renaissance villa. And 'the way a building works' could mean several different things, such as the way it stands up, the way it allows certain activities to take place within it and around it, or the way it modifies environmental conditions, keeping its interior warm or cool, for example. Responsible architects are these days acutely conscious of the need to save energy, reduce pollution and limit the potentially catastrophic effects of global warming. Nevertheless, in hot climates the most common way to keep a building comfortably cool is still to install a mechanical air conditioner that uses lots of energy and indirectly emits lots of carbon dioxide. This is a non-organic approach to environmental modification. The organic approach would be to control the temperature passively, by shading the walls of the building under big roof overhangs or behind louvred screens, and by encouraging the flow of cooling air by means of wind towers. And there are corresponding techniques for cold climates: high levels of insulation, conservatories that trap the heat of the winter sun, and heavy walls and floors that soak up and store that heat, releasing it slowly to take the chill off the cold night. These are called 'passive' technologies because they use only the free, non-polluting energy of the sun, but we could also call them 'organic' technologies because they are formal adaptations to climatic conditions, like the fur of an arctic fox or the hump of a camel.

The Eden Project, built in a redundant china-clay quarry in Cornwall and designed by Nicholas Grimshaw, is organic in several ways. Its function is to display plants from all over the world, not as individual specimens but in combinations that recreate the natural ecologies into which they fit. The buildings that house these displays are called 'biomes' (biological domes). They are really just greenhouses but so big that they seem more like complete self-sufficient environments – a space station on a hostile planet, perhaps. It is hard to describe these structures without immediately resorting to organic similes. They look like honeycombs, or insects' eyes, or frogspawn, or some kind of weirdly fruiting fungus. They are also like bubbles, attaching themselves to the floor and wall of the clay pit and joined, as bubbles often are, by perfect semicircular arches. Their natural or organic visual character seems genuinely to arise from the organic principles of their design. For one thing, they are extremely efficient in structural terms. The spans are enormous but the steel rods and nodes that form the hexagons and

The 'biomes' of the Eden Project in Cornwall, designed by Nicholas Grimshaw, are organic in several ways. They look like organisms – insect eyes, perhaps, or frog spawn – they contain organic displays, and they were designed by a process that imitated the processes of nature. But there is a limit to this comparison between the organic and the man-made. The biomes did not grow; they were erected painstakingly on a massive scaffold.

pentagons of the framework are light enough to be manhandled. There are organic irregularities too, where the bubbles meet the ground. Here the architects consciously followed the example of the dragonfly's wing in which a hexagonal pattern of veins adapts itself in an ad hoc way where it meets a leading edge or a structural spar. Even the 'glass' of the greenhouses is like an organic membrane, not glass at all but a new plastic material called ETFE made into triple-layer inflated cushions.

What we learn from this example is that the conceptually organic and the visually organic often go together. Sometimes it's hard to separate the two. Did the architect of the Eden Project deliberately make the biomes look like honeycombs and dragonfly wings or do organic forms like these tend to arise naturally whenever an architect or an engineer tries to make an efficient structure? Perhaps efficient structures tend to look organic because nature always uses efficient structures. The architect was not imitating the natural form the way a painter or a sculptor might, he was imitating a natural form-making process. It is time to take a closer look at nature's form-making processes and see to what extent they are paralleled by form-making processes in architecture.

Natural forms

In order to imitate consciously the form-making processes of nature, an architect would first have to know something about those processes. This seems an obvious point but it is important because it recognizes the distinction between what nature is really like and what we think it is like – our imperfect knowledge of it. Such is the prestige of modern science that we tend to think that practically everything is known about nature. Ask a genuine scientist, however, and he or she will tell you that our knowledge of nature is always provisional, always changing, and will probably continue to change as long as there are scientists around to formulate theories, conduct research, and disagree with one another. In ancient Greece, philosophers formulated theories about the world around them, including theories about form and matter and how things were made. As we saw in Chapter 3, Plato separated form from matter and made form the dominant partner. Pure form existed only as an ideal in the mind of God, and the actual forms seen in nature were but pale reflections of those ideal forms. So God took the unformed matter of the Earth and imposed form upon it. Form was 'transcendent'. For later Judaeo–Christian and Muslim philosophers this theory seemed to conform to mythical accounts of the creation of the world in which form was God-given and unchanging. In nature, therefore, form-making was a top-down thing. What do we think now? Ever since Charles Darwin's conceptual breakthrough 150 years ago – the idea that species evolved over millions of years by the process of natural selection and survival of the fittest – the orthodox view has been that organic form emerges from the process of evolution. It is not 'transcendent' but 'immanent', not above nature but within nature, not top-down but bottom-up.

Over the past 40 years or so, connections between real philosophy and architectural theory have strengthened, and lately one branch of philosophy in particular has begun to exert an influence, directly or indirectly, over those architects who are interested in the relationship between architecture and nature. The French philosopher, Gilles Deleuze, who died in 1995, tackled a bewildering range of topics, and for anyone other than a professional philosopher his books, some of them written in collaboration with Felix Guattari, are extraordinarily hard to read. Luckily the part of his philosophy that tries to describe what it is to be in the world – his 'ontology' – can be simplified in ways that make it useful to architectural theory. But as a preparation for Deleuze, we should first look at a biology book which was written almost a hundred years ago and has been an inspiration to organic architects ever since.

On Growth and Form, by the Scottish biologist, D'Arcy Wentworth Thompson, is a descriptive rather than a theoretical work. It describes not just the forms of organisms but the relationships, especially the mathematical relationships, between those forms and the forces at work in the environment in which they evolved. For example, it describes how the 'principle of similitude' controls the sizes of animals and plants. When the dimensions of an object are changed, the surface area and volume of that object also change, but not at the same rate. So, when the radius of a sphere is doubled, its surface area is quadrupled, but its volume, and therefore its weight if it is a solid object of uniform density, is multiplied by eight. In other words, the surface area increases as the square, and the volume as the cube of the radius. 'From these elementary principles,' says D'Arcy Thompson, 'a great many consequences follow.'[2] This is an understatement. The principle of similitude explains why there are no land animals bigger than an elephant, why small animals move quickly and large animals slowly, why there are no mammals smaller than a shrew but no insects bigger than a Goliath beetle, and why the trunks of pine trees taper gracefully upwards. This obviously has important implications for architects and engineers. D'Arcy Thompson actually uses the example of steel girder as a simple illustration of the principle, coming to the surprising conclusion (surprising to architects if not to engineers) that of two geometrically similar bridges, the larger will be the weaker.

Another chapter of the book, devoted to comparisons of closely related organisms, is illustrated by fascinating line drawings which show, with startling clarity, how, for example, the outward form of a particular species of fish can be transformed into that of a completely different species of fish by means of a simple geometrical distortion. D'Arcy Thompson probably never heard the word 'morphing' but were he alive now he would surely be making use of that computer animation technique that turns one persons face into another, or a horse into a rabbit. Two thoughts emerge from a contemplation of these transformations. The first is that the two species of fish are in one sense physically very different – one is long and thin, the other short and fat – but in another sense very similar in that both have the same inventory of features such as fins, tails, eyes, gills and so on. The second is that the transformation, that is the very gradual evolution from one species to another through the mechanism of natural selection, has taken place because of a change in the conditions in which the organism is obliged to live – a change in the temperature or salinity of the water, for example, or in the location of the food supply so that the fish is forced to swim at

Illustrations from D'Arcy Wentworth Thompson's book *On Growth and Form*, first published in 1917. The various fishes are topologically similar, that is they have similar inventories of components arranged in similar ways; but they are metrically dissimilar – some are short and fat, others long and thin. These metrical differences between species are caused by differences in their habitats. Could buildings imitate this method of form-finding?

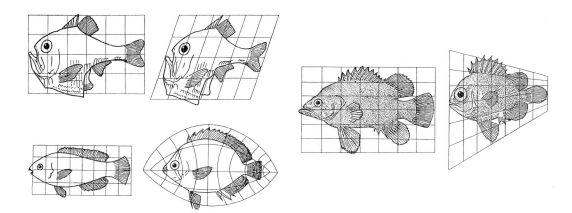

a greater depth where the pressure is higher and sunlight dimmer. And immediately we are thinking about the world and nature in a way that is similar to Deleuze's way of thinking. Our guide to Deleuze's ontology is Manuel DeLanda, who specializes in explaining Deleuze to non-philosophers and to architects in particular.[3]

Extended and intensive forms

According to Deleuze, 'everything which happens and everything which appears is correlated with orders of differences: differences of level, temperature, pressure, tension, potential, differences of intensity.'[4] This concept of intensity is important. When we think about 'morphogenesis' – form and the way that it appears in the world – we tend to think about static form, form as envisaged by Plato, form that is imposed upon matter from above. We might call this 'extended' form because it is extended in space. But for Deleuze this is a naïve illusion. The extensive world, he says, can never in reality be separated from the intensive world – the world of forces, temperatures, pressures, speeds and chemical concentrations.

The extensive and the intensive have completely different characteristics. An extended form can be divided quantitatively with predictable results. For example, if a cubic metre (35.3 cubic feet) of water is divided in half, the result will be two half cubic metres of water. The halving of the volume of the water will not, however, halve its temperature. The temperature may well change slightly because of the energy used in the halving of the volume, but the half volumes will not be half as hot as the original volume. Extended form – the form that Plato was interested in – is easy to manipulate and control because, conceptually at least, it is inert. Intensities are hard to control because they are by nature dynamic. And what makes them dynamic is difference. If heat is applied to a vessel full of water – a kettle on a stove – the difference of temperature between the top and bottom of the kettle will cause the water to move. Convection currents will be observed as the colder water sinks and displaces the water that has been warmed by the stove. These convection currents will take a particular form – perhaps rising around the walls of the vessel and sinking in the centre. As the intensity – the temperature – increases, the form of the convection changes, becoming more turbulent until a critical threshold is reached and it begins to boil. If we put the kettle in the deep freeze, the form of the water will eventually change into what appears to be completely different substance: ice. Intensities therefore act on matter to produce form. A weather map is a good illustration of this. The base map of the land and its borders with the sea represents extended form, remaining the same from day to day. The map of the atmosphere that overlays it represents differing intensities of temperature and pressure and the forms made by those differences – the cyclones and anticyclones, the ridges and troughs of pressure, the warm and cold fronts. This part of the map changes every day, every minute.

Note that we have begun to talk about inorganic as well as organic form. For Deleuze this distinction is not as clear cut as it is in common parlance. All matter for him is alive with morphogenetic potential. The 'birth' and 'growth' of a hurricane in the Caribbean is not so different in principle from the birth and growth of an animal. And the animal is not an isolated specimen to be dissected and analysed by zoologists, but part of an infinitely complex whole that includes not just its ecological setting – the food it eats and the other animals that prey on it – but the very ground on which it walks. In certain special cases the morphogenetic potential of matter becomes clearly apparent because of the geometrical regularity of the forms produced. Symmetrical crystals, the facetted columns of basalt rock formations and the perfect spheres of soap bubbles are cases in point. Perhaps it was these phenomena that led thinkers of the past to place greater importance on regular than irregular forms, to imagine, as Plato did, that tetrahedrons, cubes, octahedrons and icosahedrons were in some way fundamental to the structure of the universe. For Deleuze this favouring of regular forms is a mistake. Forms always have to be understood in terms of the underlying differences in intensity that produced them. The forces acting in a film of soapy water that contains a body of air will naturally resolve themselves into an equilibrium state that minimizes surface tension. It is not the resulting perfect sphere that is important, however, but the dynamic process that produced it.

The question of regularity introduces another important aspect of Deleuze's ontology. Regular forms are metrical forms. Forms such as spheres, cubes and tetrahedrons are classified and named according to their metrical similarities, the fixed ratios between their physical dimensions. This metrical way of dealing with forms is sometimes called Euclidean geometry after the ancient Greek mathematician. But there are other geometries, other ways of classifying and naming forms. Projective geometry is one such. If you cut a square hole in a

Perspective is a form of projective geometry. In this diagram, the square on the wall becomes distorted by the angled picture plane – in other words by the position of the viewer. The square and its representation are not identical but are nevertheless considered to be equivalent in projective geometry.

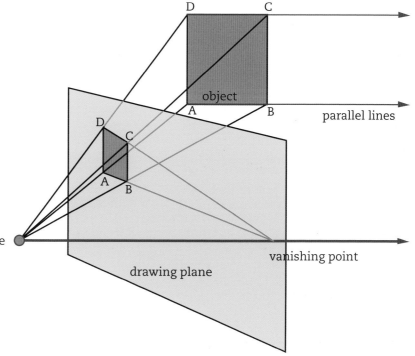

piece of cardboard and shine a light through it onto a wall, taking care to keep everything straight, then a square patch of light will appear on the wall. But if the sheet of cardboard is tilted, the patch of light will be distorted into a shape which, though recognizably akin to the original square, has quite different angles and proportions. The original square belongs to Euclidean geometry, but the distorted square belongs to projective geometry. In the latter, all of the possible distorted squares produced by the apparatus are considered to be equivalent, not just those with matching angles and proportions. Projective geometry is familiar to artists and architects because it is the basis of perspective representation.

In another type of geometry, 'topology', forms are said to be similar not because they visually resemble one another but because the space they occupy has a similar pattern of connectivity. The best example to illustrate this is an experiment carried out by one of the pioneers in the development of topology, Leonhard Euler.[5] Euler discovered that the city of Konigsberg was configured in such a way that it was impossible to plan a route through it that crossed all of its seven bridges just once. We don't need to examine the plan in detail to realize that it would be possible to find, or perhaps design, another city that, though completely different in other respects – its size, its rivers, its hills, whether its streets were straight or winding – nevertheless shared this pattern of connectedness. In Euclidean terms the second city would be different, but in topological terms it would be the same. Extending this thought a little further, we can perhaps envisage other forms or spaces that are different in one geometry but similar in another. We are reminded of D'Arcy Thompson's drawings and of the way that they morph into one another. The skull of an elephant can become the skull of a crocodile because, although metrically they are completely different, topologically they are equivalent. Now put this together will the concept of intensity and difference and we can perhaps glimpse, at least in a rudimentary way, how morphogenesis works in Deleuze's ontology and how it differs from older concepts of form-making.

Form, whether organic or inorganic, soap bubble or crocodile, arises from topological configurations of intensities which, in Manuel DeLanda's words, 'inhabit spaces of energetic possibilities'.[6] In what sense these configurations and spaces can be said to 'exist' is a difficult philosophical question. But then so is the question of the existence of the old Platonic forms. Deleuze tends to avoid the words 'possible' and 'real', preferring instead the words 'virtual' and 'actual'. So beneath the world of actual form lies a virtual, dynamic world full of form-making potential. The important thing is that form is not imposed from above, but is immanent in matter and energy. And it arises not from some kind of copying process that would fix the form for ever, but from an open-ended morphogenesis that is always changing. One example of this constant change is evolution.

The architecture–nature relationship

It may be something of a relief to return now to the more tangible world of architecture. How different does it look after this rough

sketch of the ontology of Gilles Deleuze? We saw how the design
of the Eden Project was influenced not just by the forms of nature,
including bubbles, but also the processes of nature. We know a little
more about those processes now and perhaps we see more clearly
the potential of the architecture/nature relationship. Encouragingly,
to illustrate this relationship, Manuel DeLanda chooses examples that
are already familiar from recent architectural history. One of these is
the work of the great Catalan architect of the early twentieth century,
Antoni Gaudí.[7] Gaudí was unquestionably an organic architect. His
buildings were inspired by the forms of animals and plants and also, as
we shall see, by natural morphogenetic principles. Look, for example,
at the chapel he built for Colònia Güell, a workers' colony at Santa
Coloma de Cervelló. Only the crypt was finished before the project was
abandoned in 1914. The structure might loosely be described as Gothic
but this is not the ordered, hierarchical Gothic of the Middle Ages, still
less its rationalized nineteenth-century version. Columns seem to be
dotted about randomly and they all slope in different directions as if
contorting themselves in a desperate attempt to hold up the tangled
and twisted net of the vault ribs. Some columns are brick piers, some
are of rough-hewn stone. The interior is less like a pine forest than a
gutted animal carcass. Materials, mainly brick, stone and concrete, are
mixed according to no discernible logic. In the external walls, fairly
regular, coursed brickwork suddenly gives way to over-burnt rejects
simply piled up and stuck together with mortar. This tends to happen
under the teardrop shaped windows making them look like the weeping
eyes of some giant reptile.

So much for the organic form – but what about the morphogenetic
principles? The idea is simple but brilliant. Gaudí did not so much
imitate nature as collaborate with it. As we have seen, in a vaulted
Gothic structure the key to stability is to conduct all of the forces
– the weight of the stones and the pressure of the wind – down to
the foundations through a combination of vault-ribs, columns and
buttresses. The vault-ribs tend to push the columns over, but the
buttresses balance this force and maintain stability. Gaudí realized that
the force could be balanced in another way: by sloping the columns
so that they, as it were, leant against the pressure of the vault. By
abandoning the masons' instinct for verticality, he freed the form of
the building from conventional architectural order. Structural members
could now follow the forces wherever they led. He also realized that
there was a simple, natural way to visualize the forces so that the
members could be positioned in line with them. He simply imagined
that the compressive forces were tension forces and mapped them in
an upside down weighted string model. As long as the weights were
proportional to the forces in the actual building, the strings would
indicate the most efficient positions for the structural members.
Substituting solid members for strings and turning the model the right
way up automatically established the most efficient configuration. It
was not so much form-making as form-finding.

The technique was also applied in the building for which Gaudí
is best known, the Sagrada Familia Church in Barcelona, the scale of
which matches the great medieval cathedrals. In the crypt museum

of the church, one of Gaudí's big weighted string models has been reconstructed and can be compared with the building itself, a building which, more than 100 years after its commencement, is still under construction. There is a crucial difference, however, between the new parts of the building and those parts that were completed in Gaudí's lifetime. Gaudí's structure was truly Gothic in that it consisted only of un-reinforced stone. The new structure is of reinforced concrete, which has a fundamentally different material and structural character. The precise balancing of forces is no longer necessary and the weighted string model has become irrelevant. The building is still organic in appearance, but it is no longer organic in construction.

Manuel DeLanda points out that the morphogenetic principle behind Gaudí's models is, in Deleuze's terms, the same as that which produces soap bubbles.[8] When a chain hangs loosely from two fixed ends, it automatically adopts a catenary curve that minimizes the potential energy of the gravitational forces acting on the chain. Topologically speaking, this is the same process by which soap films minimise surface tension and form perfectly spherical bubbles. There is nothing organic, in the sense of biological, about this; the potential for form-making is immanent in the materials and the topological configuration of intensities, in this case structural forces. But the process of morphogenesis in plants and animals is in principle the same. The growth of a human embryo, for example, unfolds, cell by cell, from the

The Sagrada Familia in Barcelona by Antoni Gaudí (above left). The parts of the church that were completed in Gaudí's lifetime was built in un-reinforced stone but the later phases (it is still under construction) were built in reinforced concrete. The organic essence of the building has therefore been destroyed.

One of the hanging models that Gaudí used to 'find' the forms of his buildings (above right). The little bags of lead represent the loads acting on the building and the strings represent the structural members. When the photograph is turned upside down, tension becomes compression and an efficient structural form emerges.

progressive resolution of similar topological configurations of intensities, this time guided by the inherited genetic code of the DNA molecule.

The virtual diagram

The analogy between natural morphogenesis and form-making in architecture is clearest when we are considering the engineering aspects of the building – structure or heating and ventilation. In a sense engineers are always collaborating with nature. They can't ignore gravity and thermodynamics. But what about the less constrained aspects of the form of a building – its plan, for example? Does the topological and intensive way of thinking have any relevance to this area of design? In a sense, most practical design methods can be seen in terms of natural morphogenesis. When an architect establishes a brief for a building, he or she will ask the client about the sorts of activity that will take place in it, the numbers of people involved, the sizes of the groups, how they will be distributed over time, and so on. We might call these intensities of use. And perhaps the first drawing that the architect makes will be some kind of bubble or flow diagram to represent the different uses and the necessary connections between them. If it is a school, for example, then the diagram might represent the relationships between the classrooms, the assembly hall and the playground. The diagram will not be to scale because it represents connectivity, not quantity. In other words, it is a topological diagram. So the architect deals with topologies and intensities just as nature does.

The final form of the building will be the actualization in extended space of these virtual diagrams. Modern architects have been Deleuzians all along it seems. When we combine the plan with the structure, and the heating and ventilation system, including the external walls and roofs, all designed according to organic principles, we have an organic piece of architecture, whether or not it looks anything like a natural organism. The snag is, though, that we have separated these different parts of the design, giving each a distinct form, sometimes even making a different designer responsible for each part. Architects are expected to know something about structural principles, but the handing over of an outline design to a structural consultant so that he or she can 'engineer it' is still a very common way to proceed. Nature doesn't do this. Nature seems to design things all at once. Components of organisms are not added one to another, like walls added to floors and roofs added to walls, they are integrated into the whole that we call an organism. How can architecture achieve this wholeness, this continuity, this smoothness?

The answer is computers. In recent years, computer-aided design (CAD) programs have been developed that allow the architect to manipulate form directly in three dimensions. Often this involves the progressive distortion and elaboration of an original simple form such as a cube or a sphere. This might explain the rash of blob-like buildings that appeared in the late 1990s as architects became proficient in CAD programs and began to free themselves from the traditional plan–section–elevation, wall–floor–roof way of thinking. But the real potential of these programs became clear only when 'scripting' components were added to them. Suddenly an exciting new possibility opened up: the automatic design of buildings, sometimes called 'algorithmic' or

Natural form 'emerges' spontaneously from shifting combinations of influential factors. This cloud in the sky over Rome is made of thousands of small organisms (starlings) but we could also look upon it as a single organism with a single, dynamic form. Parametric or algorithmic design aims to produce architectural form by a similar process.

'parametric' design. An algorithm is like a recipe, a set of instructions for the creation of something new, such as a steak and kidney pie or a building. But whereas with a recipe the result is (we hope) predictable – a recipe for a steak and kidney pie will not produce a chocolate cake – the whole point of an algorithm is that we are willing to be surprised. We want it to find a novel form, not some traditional form that we already knew about. If we have a particular problem to solve – to find the most efficient circulation plan for a school, perhaps – we devise an algorithm that tells the computer to test all the possible plans and find the one that uses the shortest length of corridor. This is the kind of thing that computers are good at. We probably won't use the plan precisely as designed by the computer because it might not be very beautiful (beauty is the kind of thing computers are not good at), but knowing the optimum solution will surely help us to arrive at a satisfactory design.

Similarly, an algorithm might be devised to find the best layout for an estate of standard houses, taking into account the requirements for access, privacy, sunlight, gradient, etc. The computer will test all the possible layouts until it finds the one that maximizes the number of houses without breaking any of the rules or limits set by the algorithm. Such a procedure might well produce interesting formal regularities such as parallel streets or branching hierarchies or star-shaped clusters. These 'emergent' forms would be the equivalent of soap bubbles and crystals, or of the extraordinarily beautiful curved and folded shapes made in the evening sky by flocks of starlings as they gather to roost. In nature, all form is 'emergent'; nothing is 'designed'. Algorithmic design is an attempt to steal some of the magic of emergent form by imitating nature's processes.

In these examples, the task is relatively easy to define and quantify but what if we want to include more factors, such as the sizes of the school classrooms or the design of the windows of the houses? The equations become very much more complex. Add in the choice of materials (including their cost, their durability and their structural characteristics), the load-bearing capacity of the soil, energy consumption, daylight requirements, perhaps even a few aesthetic prejudices – all of the factors that human designers have to consider – and even the computer begins to struggle. It needs guidance; it needs limits; it can't cope with infinite choice. It must have a starting point, a precedent, some kind of morphogenetic system.

Architects working in the still mainly experimental field of algorithmic design turn to nature for guidance when devising morphogenetic systems for their computers to work with. The kind of articulated, metrical form that is typical of conventional buildings does not occur much in plants and animals, at least not in those parts of plants and animals that divide and contain, like the skin of a mammal, for example. Skin tends to be continuous and curvaceous, adapting itself to the movement of the animal and to changing environmental conditions: shivering when it gets cold, sweating when it gets hot. And different parts of the body are covered in different kinds of skin – soft and thin where protected in bodily crevices, but hard and thick on feet or hands. Microscopically, skin, like the rest of the animal, is made of cells. Cells start out all the same in the embryo ('stem cells') but become specialized as the animal grows and the distinct forms of its bones, muscles and organs emerge. This combination of curved surface and cellular structure is a typical starting point for the computer-designed buildings that are beginning to lay claim to the territory known as 'organic architecture'. The curved surface is capable of adapting itself to its environment and its functional program much more flexibly than a traditional rectilinear architectural element: it can be floor, wall and ceiling combined. And the cellular structure allows for differentiation of surface type. The man-made cells are not microscopic but of a scale that makes them visible and handle-able, like windows and doors. Cells can vary in profile, thickness, load-bearing capacity, insulating value, transparency, and any number of other qualities, in response to changes in the environmental conditions or changes in the surrounding cells. They might incorporate some dynamic or even mechanical feature, such as photosensitive glass or ventilation apertures that open and close, but even if they are static and fixed they can all be different, each cell responding to the unique environment of its precise location. It is hard to find built examples of this kind of organic building because the

Zaha Hadid's design for a performing arts centre in Abu Dhabi is a good example of the kind of curvaceous form that emerges from the process of parametric design. But is the animal-like form of the building the natural outcome of the design process or is there some extrinsic, cultural force at work – fashion, for example? This is architecture; it can never be completely natural.

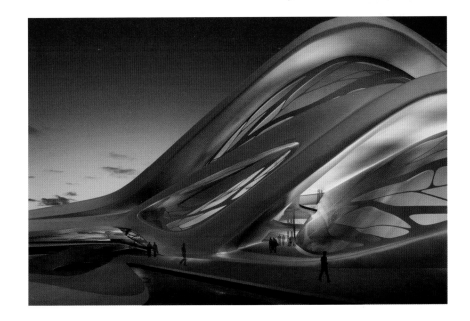

computer-aided machines necessary to make them are still relatively rare in the building industry, but we can get a good idea of how they might look from thousands of unbuilt schemes, student projects and demonstration pieces in exhibitions.

Meanwhile, in the real world simple versions are beginning to appear, such as the famous 'bird's nest' Olympic stadium in Beijing, which could never have been built in pre-digital times, or the glass roof of the Great Court at the British Museum in London, which has a form like a swelling soap film supported by a delicate space frame of steel bars and nodes which are all different. In the past, such structures had to be made from a limited range of standard components in order to avoid repeated retooling which would have been prohibitively time-consuming and expensive. Now, computer-controlled machines can be adjusted instantly so the old imperative to standardize has disappeared. It is perhaps this development more than any other that has made possible the modern revival of the organic approach to design.

Evolution and design

So, given the right algorithm and the right set of parameters, a computer can design a building almost the way that nature 'designs' an animal or a plant, that is to say by finding forms that are fit for the environment. The building will behave organically, and it will probably also look organic. But there is a rather important natural process that is missing from this comparison: evolution. Can computers also mimic evolution? Actually, computers have been mimicking evolution for decades, creating various primitive forms of 'artificial life' using so-called genetic algorithms, and there is no reason in principle why designs for buildings should not be produced in this way. After all, the concept of architectural evolution is hardly new. The general idea that building types and styles evolve over long periods of time goes back to the nineteenth century and even predates the publication of Darwin's *On the Origin of Species* in 1859. For example, James Fergusson, in his *True Principles of Beauty in Art*, published in 1849, recommends the following method by which the perfect design for an Anglo-Protestant church might be evolved: run a competition for the design of the church, build the winning design, note its defects and put them right in the next church to be built; then repeat the process until the perfect design is arrived at. Fergusson estimates that about ten iterations of the process ought to do the trick.

Post-Darwinian ideas of evolution are less naïve. We have seen how topological and intensive forms of thought are necessary for a Deleuzian understanding of natural morphogenesis. In order to understand how evolution works in nature we must add a third point of view – populational thinking.[9] Evolution in nature is more than just a step-by-step process of improvement that eventually leads to an optimal solution. Rather, it is a phenomenon that emerges from the relationship between a large population of individuals and a given environment. Optimization is not involved. The whole point of Darwinian evolution is that it is purposeless. It may be reasonable to say that one of the causes of the creation of a building is the final building, which does not yet exist but towards which the creative process is nevertheless progressing. This is an ancient, Aristotelian idea, sometimes called the 'final' or

The bird's nest stadium, designed by Herzog and de Meuron for the 2008 Beijing Olympics. This building could never have been built in pre-digital times. It would have been necessary to standardize the structural components in order to make the calculations manageable and the production economical. Now, computers cope easily with variety and difference.

'teleological' cause. But evolution has no such cause, only an effect: the survival of the fittest. A random mutation in the genetic code of a species appears in an individual and if it happens to confer a survival advantage then that individual will reproduce successfully and pass on the advantage to future generations.

It is hard to see any convincing parallel between this blind, emergent process and the deliberate act of architectural design. For one thing, modern architects are used to the idea that invention and novelty, though rare, are at least possible. But nature doesn't invent anything new. It always develops something existing; its basic orientation is more towards the past than the future. All that evolution does is very slowly make minor modifications to long-established 'body plans' – the skeletons of mammals, for example, which, though they may vary widely from species to species, are topologically similar. This is not much like architecture as we know it. If genetic algorithms are to have any application in architectural design it will be necessary to intervene in the 'automatic' design process in some very artificial ways such as creating populations, choosing suitable body plans and deliberately introducing 'random' mutations. The results might still be interesting, but it is long way from nature. Despite the temptingly lifelike qualities of the products of digital design, the phrase 'organic architecture' is still only an analogy, as it always has been.

CHAPTER 7
HISTORY

Why do architecture students study architectural history? Training courses for other professions, like medicine or engineering, do not usually involve history lessons, so why do most respectable university architecture courses include quite generous allocations of time to the subject? Sometimes it is given a different name – 'cultural context' is a popular alternative – but typically it involves a 'survey course' in first year, which outlines the history of architecture from ancient Egypt to present day, followed by a more concentrated second year course in the history of modern architecture, and then a requirement in third year to write some kind of history dissertation. Most of the students on the course are hoping to become architects, not historians, so why do they need all this history? What can the modern designer learn, in a practical sense, from the study of Roman temples or Gothic cathedrals or Renaissance palaces? Surely they are too remote, chronologically and culturally, to be relevant to current architectural practice?

There is a practical kind of architectural history called a 'precedent study' that is considered immediately applicable to current practice. If you are designing a school it obviously makes sense to look at the schools that other architects have designed. But it also makes sense to keep an open mind about the form that the proposed school might take and to draw on a wide range of precedents, including examples of other building types from other places and periods – in other words to study architectural history. And surely it would seem strange if the designers of modern buildings knew nothing about those old buildings that society has chosen to preserve, that we still use and that, perhaps, we have grown to love. We live in and among old buildings and their very presence excites curiosity. If we want to understand the meaning of a Gothic cathedral, or how it was built and how it stands up, it seems natural to ask an architect. Perhaps the link between architectural history and architectural practice is simply a function of the tendency of buildings, especially symbolically important buildings like cathedrals, to endure for long periods of time.

These are good practical and social reasons why architects should study the buildings of the past, and yet they seem to miss something essential about the relationship between architecture and history. Before we explore this further, we should be clear what we mean by 'history'. Sometimes the word is used to mean simply 'the past' – the events that took place in a former time – and sometimes it is used to refer to the activity of investigating the past – what historians do, the creation and maintenance of the historical record. In the first sense, history (the past) is an inescapable dimension of every field of human creativity, including art, science, technology and language. We use the rather misleading word 'tradition' to refer to this dimension but all we mean is that, in practice and perhaps also in principle, nothing created by human beings is ever completely new. There is always an existing 'cultural context' into which the created work has to fit. Tradition is always present, if only as something to be denied or reacted against. For example, the house as a building type is often said to have been 're-invented' by progressive architects who reject every traditional domestic form, space, material or ornament. Ben van Berkel and Caroline Bos's Möbius House in Utrecht seems like a completely new architectural form – a dynamic spatial loop through which the sequence of human uses travels on a daily basis. But it is still a house, it still calls itself a house, it still accommodates domestic activities like eating, resting and sleeping, and its published plans still bear labels like 'living room', 'bedroom' and 'bathroom'. The relationship between architecture and history, in the sense of 'the past', is arguably no weaker now than it ever was.

But what about the relationship between architecture and history in the sense of a scholarly discipline? Because buildings are large, complex and durable objects we tend to rely on them in our investigations of the past. For historians they are 'primary sources' and they don't have to be looked up in libraries and archives; there they are, standing before us and around us, waiting to be analyzed and interpreted. We feel that we have learnt something about ancient Rome just by spending an hour exploring the ruins of the Colosseum, or about eighteenth-century London just by walking round a Georgian square. We feel in touch, almost literally, with the people that built these buildings, with their preferences and priorities, their sensibilities and their view of the world. Some buildings also seem to be the products of historical investigations – almost the equivalent of history books. The Gothic Revival buildings of the nineteenth century, for example, were works of scholarship as much as works of architecture. They were imaginative evocations or re-creations of certain aspects of medieval life. They served a purpose in the present but they were also contributions to a body of knowledge about the past. And the revival of classical architecture in the Renaissance was perhaps also a historical project of a kind, an attempt to bring back to life the golden age of ancient Rome. These are examples of architecture conceived as a form of historical knowledge.

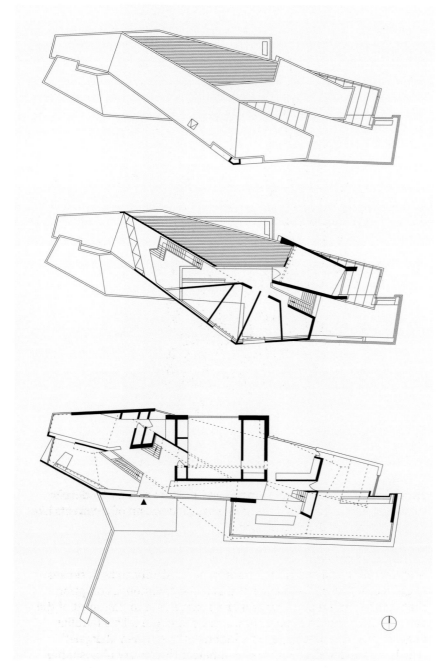

The Möbius House (1998) by Ben van Berkel and Caroline Bos seems anything but traditional. Plans show how its spaces flow in a continuous loop or möbius strip, following the diurnal pattern of human use. But it still accommodates ordinary activities like eating, sleeping and talking to one another; and it is still called a 'house'.

Twentieth-century Modernist architects dismissed the nineteenth-century revivals as irrelevant to a progressive, forward-looking industrial culture, but before long Modernism itself was being revived. In the 1970s, a group of architects known as the New York Five began to build and publish projects that paid homage to the abstract beauty of the pioneer Modernist architecture of the 1920s. One of the group, Richard Meier, designed beautifully proportioned pure white houses, such as the Douglas House in Harbour Springs, Michigan, that were clearly developments and refinements of Le Corbusier's Purist villas. Certain

Gothic Revival buildings of the nineteenth century were works of historical scholarship as well as works of architecture. Architecture and history seemed then to be inseparable. The drawing represents Viollet-le-Duc's 'ideal' Gothic cathedral. But there is a paradox here: one can copy every aspect of past style except its originality.

critics began to refer to this kind of architecture as 'neo-Modernist' to distinguish it from the emerging post-Modernism of architects like Robert Venturi and Charles Moore.

The spirit of the age

Architecture has a special relationship with history, in both senses of the word. One consequence of this is the common assumption that architecture represents and gives expression to 'the spirit of the age', the fundamental beliefs of a society or culture. This familiar English phrase is actually a translation of the German 'Zeitgeist' which is associated with the early nineteenth-century philosopher Georg Wilhelm Friedrich Hegel. Hegel saw the history of nations as a succession of cultures or ages that were born, flourished and died like living beings.[1] And like living beings, each had a soul or spirit (Geist). Later nineteenth-century thinkers took this idea and applied it to the history of art, including architecture. The architecture of the past started to be looked upon not as a continuing tradition within which the architects of the present inevitably worked, but as a succession of distinctive styles each expressing the spirit of the age. Styles were given names like Gothic, Renaissance, Mannerist and Baroque. These terms have become so familiar that we tend to forget they were all

Even architecture that seems completely modern has a historical dimension. The houses of Richard Meier (illustrated here is the Saltzman House of 1969) borrow freely from the Purism of Le Corbusier's pre-war villas.

coined retrospectively by historians. Bernini, Borromini and Guarini did not know that they were Baroque architects because the term Baroque was not applied to the florid classical buildings of the seventeenth century until the early nineteenth century. And, like many of these stylistic names, it was originally a pejorative term, meaning irregularly shaped, grotesque or odd. Similarly Gothic originally meant barbarous and uncouth and was not applied to medieval architecture until the late eighteenth century. (It has nothing whatever to do with the Goths, one of the Germanic tribes that invaded parts of the Roman Empire from the second century onwards.)

In this Hegelian version of architectural history, each style or age is subdivided into phases that roughly correspond to the phases of a creative human life. In its youth the style might be vigorous and inventive, but relatively primitive; in its prime it will be at the height of its powers, producing its great works; in its later years it will inevitably decline, becoming lazy and self-indulgent. So, the simplicity and clarity of the early Renaissance (Brunelleschi, perhaps) is supplanted by the total command and subtle refinement of the 'high' Renaissance (Bramante and Raphael) which in turn is supplanted by the decadence of late Renaissance Mannerism (Giulio Romano).

This is all very well as a convenient way to classify the buildings of the past, but we must bear in mind that it is an abstract structure imposed on the historical evidence after the fact and that it can only ever be provisional. Other interpretations are always possible. We might decide, for example, that historical periods are not much like human lives, that they don't rise and fall or grow and decay and that they don't have spirits. The Hegelian view is questionable and becomes even more so when it is applied not to the past but to the present. It is one thing to see a building as an expression of the spirit of a past age, quite another to require a new building to express the spirit of the present age. But this is what modern architects, historians and theorists tend to do.

Sigfried Giedion was the Modern Movement's in-house historian and an exponent of the Hegelian historical method. He explained his method very clearly in the introduction to his best-known book, *Space, Time and Architecture*, first published in 1941. He begins by acknowledging the influence of his teacher, the Swiss art historian, Heinrich Wölfflin:

> 'In our personal contacts with him as well as through his distinguished lectures, we, his pupils, learned to grasp the spirit of an epoch.'[2]

So there is the familiar phrase – 'spirit of the epoch' – and the clear implication that, in order to understand the past, a historian must grasp that spirit. But Giedion was more than just a historian; he was also an apologist for, and promoter of, the emerging Modernist style of architecture. For him the most important epoch was the present epoch. He goes on to make a bold assertion about the very nature of history:

> 'The historian, the historian of architecture especially, must be in close contact with contemporary conceptions. Only when he is permeated by the spirit of his own time is he prepared to detect those aspects of the past which previous generations have overlooked.'[3]

This is a reversal of what we might expect. According to Giedion, we don't study the past in order to understand the present; we study the present in order to understand the past. There is a special word to describe this way of looking at the past: 'teleological', which means, roughly, 'with the benefit of hindsight'. Teleology is something that historians would normally wish to avoid. If the historian's aim is to understand how people in the past thought about themselves and their place in the world, then a knowledge of subsequent events, of which they were completely ignorant, must, logically, be irrelevant. Giedion ignores this objection because he is much more interested in the present than the past. For him, the purpose of history is to find the roots of the present in the past. But before he can do that, he must first

decide what is most important about the present. In the 1930s, when he was beginning to write *Space, Time and Architecture*, Modernism by no means represented the mainstream of international architecture. It was an avant-garde movement pursued by a small intellectual elite in France, Holland and Germany and it was already under threat from the ultra conservative taste of emerging authoritarian regimes. Most architects were building in more traditional, more popular, styles even though, in other respects, their buildings were innovative. In New York, for example, Art Deco skyscrapers like the Empire State Building and the Chrysler Building were stylistically oblivious of the European Modernism that Giedion was keen to promote. Nevertheless, in Giedion's worldview it is Modernism that is most important. It may not be the style of the present, but it is the style of the future, destined eventually to triumph over the forces of conservatism. In other words, it represents the spirit of the age. His task as a historian is therefore to find the roots of Modernism in the past and this he does without much difficulty, using his teleological method. Looking back at the architecture of the nineteenth century,

The written history of twentieth-century architecture is massively biased in favour of European Modernism, but most of the important buildings – the Chrysler and Empire State buildings in New York, for example – are not Modernist at all. History is always selective and is as much influenced by the time in which it is written as the time it writes about. This is inevitable, but we must be aware of it.

he dismisses the various stylistic revivals as unimportant even though they characterized almost all public buildings. They are 'transitory facts' which 'lack the stuff of permanence and fail to attach themselves to a new tradition'. It was the undercurrents of social and technological change that were important: 'the new potentialities in construction, the use of mass production in industry, the changed organisation of society'. These are 'constituent facts' defined as 'those tendencies which, when they are suppressed, inevitably re-appear'.[4]

This is a strange kind of history. Giedion's teleology seems to work in both directions – it is a way of looking at the past but it is also a prediction of the future. He is convinced that Modernism will eventually, inevitably triumph and that it therefore represents the true spirit of the age. The only important things about the past are those hidden currents that feed the present and are destined to continue into the future. The development of frame construction in steel and reinforced concrete is just such a hidden current; stylistic revivals on the other hand are a dead end. This whole philosophical and historical edifice rests on the simple assertion that Modernism will eventually triumph, even though, at the time, this must have seemed rather unlikely. And note that the connection between Modernism and the constituent fact of frame construction is actually rather questionable. Those non-Modernist New York skyscrapers made full use of frame construction, and indeed would have been impossible to build without it.

There are fundamental philosophical objections to Giedion's idea that certain trends or potentialities in culture and society are destined to be fulfilled – in other words that that future can, in principle, be predicted. The philosopher Karl Popper, in a book called *The Poverty of Historicism*, actually presents a logical proof of the impossibility of historical prediction. The essence of his proof is:

> 'If there is such a thing as growing human knowledge, then we cannot anticipate today what we shall only know tomorrow.'[5]

If we could predict future knowledge then we would already possess it. Nothing new would ever need to be discovered and the whole enterprise of learning in general, and of science in particular, would be pointless. The implication of this proof is that the Hegelian view of history is a fantasy. If historical prediction is impossible, then the idea that history follows certain patterns – of growth and decay, for example – is also called into question because it implies a kind of retrospective prediction. We say 'that was bound to happen' only when we know that it did actually happen. If something different had happened we would probably have said that was inevitable too. Popper calls this kind of history 'historicism', which is not to be confused with the use of that term in an architectural context to mean the revival of old styles. His criticism was mainly aimed at the Marxist interpretation of history, which predicted, among other things, the inevitable eventual triumph of the proletariat over the bourgeoisie. One obvious objection to historicism is that it denies the possibility of free will. What is the point of choosing to do one thing rather than another if history has already chosen for us? But Popper's critique also has important implications for architectural

Celebration, Florida, is a new community developed by the Walt Disney Company. Most of the buildings of the world are houses, and most of these were designed and built outside the cultural field we call 'architecture'. 'Non-architectural' or 'popular' housing often adopts what Americans call a 'reminiscent' style. It seems that in the mind of the general public, architecture and history are still inseparable.

history. Belief in destiny is essential to a belief in the spirit of the age. A spirit must maintain a particular character over time in order to be a credible entity. If at any point in its emergence it might have taken a different course and shown a different character then its very existence is called into question. If 'the spirit of the age' is a meaningless phrase, then where does this leave architecture and its supposed duty to express that spirit?

Suddenly architecture's historic role is hard to believe in. Is Modernism, for example, really the true expression of the spirit of the modern age or are we being taken in by Giedion's propaganda? One might argue that Modernism triumphed only from the point of view of the narrow discipline of architectural history. General histories of architecture tend to give the impression that Modernism was the only important style of the twentieth century. In an objective view, this is very far from being the case. If we were somehow to make a complete survey of all of the buildings built in developed countries in the twentieth century we would find that only a very small proportion could reasonably be described as Modernist. Most popular housing – the wooden houses of American suburbia, for example – is stylistically completely traditional and would weight the statistics against Modernism. And throughout the twentieth century, important public buildings continued to be built in styles derived from the classical and Gothic traditions. The buildings that comprise the Lincoln Center in New York, for example, including the 1966 Metropolitan Opera House by Wallace Harrison, are surely more classical than Modernist.

The artistic canon

The truth is that architectural history, like any other kind of history, is extremely selective and often ideologically biased. And the bias tends to be reinforced by repetition. The examples a historian chooses

The Lincoln Center in New York is modern, but certainly not 'Modernist'. It is essentially classical. For some the style is dignified and appropriate, like dressing up to go to the opera; for others – especially progressive architects – it is stuffy and pompous.

to represent a particular period or country or style are recycled in subsequent histories, becoming a settled group known as the 'artistic canon'. Buildings are admitted to the canon for a variety of reasons – because they are of especially high quality, because they are innovative, or typical, or untypical, because they conform to certain prejudices, or just because a historian or journalist or photographer happens across them. There is no logical reason why admission to the canon should signify history's approval, but it usually does. A bad building might represent a period just as well as a good one but historians usually prefer to celebrate rather than denigrate. The canon is not a static list. Examples fall in and out of favour. Until the 1960s, for example, the Modernist architectural establishment, including Sigfried Giedion, tended to ignore almost all Victorian architecture on the grounds that it was fundamentally misguided. As a result, many fine buildings were ignored and some were destroyed. Now, the pendulum of taste has swung. Architects like William Butterfield, G. E. Street and Norman Shaw are considered masters from whom we can still learn, and their buildings have duly entered the canon.

The canon may be imperfect and unrepresentative but it is nevertheless useful. It provides the essential common reference points for conversations about architecture. When students pin up their designs for criticism by their teachers and peers, comparisons are sure to be made. A particular configuration of spaces will be compared to a similar arrangement in a famous building. And if the student has paid attention in history lectures, he or she will understand and benefit from the criticism.

The concept of authorship

But we must beware the considerable distortions that the canon creates. One of the most important criteria for admission to the canon is the reputation of the architect in question. Once an architect has made his or her first appearance in history, the odds are greatly in favour of further appearances. There are a few examples of architects known only for a single building – Peter Ellis's Oriel Chambers in Liverpool of 1868 comes to mind – but most canonical architects are represented by several buildings and there are a few architects whose fame is such that anything attributed to them automatically becomes 'historic'. These are the 'form-givers' and 'geniuses' of architectural history. And this is a problem. That innocent word 'attributed' conceals a thorny historical and philosophical question: the question of authorship.

Is it really possible to attribute a large, complicated work of art like a building to a single author? We might be able to say with some confidence that a painting is the work of an individual painter or a poem the work of an individual poet, but surely there are several people involved in the design of even the simplest building. The client's requirements are part of the design – it would not have taken the form it does had not the client first imagined the possibility of its existence and set the basic parameters of the project. And then there are all the design consultants – structural engineers, mechanical engineers, cost managers, not to mention builders – whose advice inevitably influences the architect's design, sometimes very radically. And we must take the size and organization of the architects' office into account. Traditionally, architects design their buildings in sketch form and pass them to assistants to work up into final, buildable designs. But it is not at all unusual for an assistant to design the building from scratch under the overall supervision of the named architect who then takes the credit. The concept of authorship is also dubious in a broader sense. Many buildings involve the building of brick walls. To what extent can an individual architect claim authorship of a brick wall? He or she might decide its profile and its dimensions and possibly certain details like the bonding pattern, but in principle the brick wall has already been designed, not by a single author but by a chain of anonymous authors forming a building tradition that stretches back hundreds of years.

Tradition itself is a kind of author. This idea has a parallel in literary criticism. When the philosopher Roland Barthes declared 'The Death of the Author' in a famous essay of 1968, he said that writing was 'the destruction of every voice, every origin'.[6] What he meant was that works of literature originate not in the minds of individual authors but in language itself, that ancient, constantly shifting field of possibilities in which writers and readers collaborate to create meaning. He wanted to break away from the kind of literary criticism that tried to 'explain' art by reference to the details of the author's life. For Barthes the person who

The Philips Pavilion at the 1958 Brussels World Fair highlights the problem of authorship in architecture. This building has been the subject of an extended monograph and has formed the centrepiece of an exhibition about Le Corbusier. But it wasn't designed by him and it was no masterpiece. The questionable habit of attributing buildings to single authors – especially if they are 'geniuses' like Le Corbusier – often distorts history and criticism.

actually did the writing was not an author, in the sense of an individual creative artist, but merely a 'scriptor', a transmitter rather than a creator of meaning. The scriptor is like the shaman in a tribal society who tells the traditional stories but takes no personal responsibility or credit for them. The parallel with architecture is not a perfect one but it nevertheless encourages us to see more clearly the complexities involved in the design of a building, how it emerges from the circumstances of its creation – the designers, the physical and cultural setting, the available materials and technologies – rather than from an exercise of individual creative will. And it makes us look in a different way at architectural history, in which authorship plays such an important part, creating and controlling the canon.

Le Corbusier is one of those form-givers whose works are all automatically canonical, even small temporary buildings like the Philips Pavilion at the 1958 Brussels World Fair. The pavilion took the form of a concrete tent in which groups of visitors gathered for a few minutes to

watch a multi-projector slide show called 'Poème électronique'. Both the building and the Poème were designed in Le Corbusier's office. It is perfectly clear, however, that they were not designed by Le Corbusier himself. The building was designed by Iannis Xenakis, Le Corbusier's assistant, who later became famous but only after he had given up architecture and made a successful career as an avant-garde composer. We should not forget also the contribution to the design made by the structural engineer, H. C. Duyster, who devised the innovative wire-stressed, precast concrete 'fabric' of the tent. The Poème was composed by the editor Jean Petit and the film-maker Philippe Agostini working with images taken from Le Corbusier's archive. The named composer of the sound track was Edgard Varèse but he could never have realized his musical vision without the assistance of the sound engineer Willem Tak. All this information comes from a 282-page book about the Philips Pavilion written by the architectural historian Mark Treib and published in 1996.[7] Such a detailed study of a relatively insignificant building would never have been carried out had not the building been attributed to Le Corbusier. Ironically, the most interesting thing that the study reveals is that the attribution is false. Looked at objectively, the Philips Pavilion was no masterpiece. In fact it was a failure. It opened a month late, its awkward form was unsuited to its function as an auditorium, its structure was over elaborate and too expensive, and visitors could only have been puzzled by the apparently random sequence of images in the Poème – a nuclear explosion, a child's face, the silhouette of a bull, a selection of urban schemes by Le Corbusier. But Le Corbusier was marginally involved in its creation, so it must take its place in history. A model of the pavilion was the focal point of a 2008 exhibition of Le Corbusier's work shown in Liverpool.[8]

The origins of authorship

Now that we have begun to question the concept of authorship it seems reasonable to ask when and where it originated. There is a clue in the way that conventional chronological surveys of architectural history are organized. When they deal with the Middle Ages, examples are usually grouped according to style – the various kinds of English Gothic architecture from Early English, through Decorated to Perpendicular, for example. But when they reach the early fifteenth century attention shifts to Italy where something called the Renaissance is said to be taking place and abruptly the system changes. Examples begin to be categorized by architect or author, and these are authors in the full sense, individuals whose biographical details are known. An important historical source is Giorgio Vasari's *Lives of the Most Excellent Painters, Sculptors and Architects*, first published in 1550, which contains biographies of 178 artists, including many important Renaissance architects such as Brunelleschi, Alberti, Bramante, Raphael, Sansovino, Peruzzi, Antonio da Sangallo, Giulio Romano and Michelangelo.

Now it is true that we also know the names of many medieval architects. We know, for example, that William of Sens designed the choir of Canterbury Cathedral and that, 200 years later, Henry Yevele and Stephen Lote designed the nave. But we don't celebrate the lives of these men or hail them as geniuses the way we do with Alberti, or Raphael or Michelangelo. We don't even think of them as architects in the modern sense. They were builders, and their power base was the mason's yard, not the studio. It is dangerous to generalize about a historical question as complex as the origins of authorship, but it seems reasonable to assume that it was during the Renaissance that the concept was fully formulated and began to be applied to architecture. And this was surely not unconnected with other developments in architecture such as the revival of ancient classical forms and the emergence of the idea of 'disegno' – design. Whereas the forms of medieval architecture had grown out of the developing technology of masonry construction, the forms of Renaissance architecture were borrowed from the past by means of scholarship and a rudimentary kind of archaeology. The relationship of these forms to construction was looser, more provisional. It was the beginning of the emancipation of architecture from construction; the beginning of the idea that architecture was an art and that it might be practised by individual artists – painters and sculptors – rather than by builders.

The relationship between architecture and history is complex. Buildings endure. They are visible, unignorable survivals from past ages. They are like time travellers, visitors from the past, and we interrogate them to find out how things used to be. But we build too, and our buildings represent us, to ourselves and to the future (which may be the same thing). When we build, we decide who we are, what is important to us and how we wish to be remembered. Our history is important to us, both in the sense of our past and of our view of the past, and architecture is involved in this aspect of our self-knowledge. It represents the continuity of a culture, even if that culture tries to reject the past, believing only in material progress. Architects study architectural history not for purely practical reasons – to help them with their designs – but because it is an integral part of the craft of architecture. The historical canon is an imperfect thing, full of distortions and injustices, in particular those created by the dubious concept of authorship and the even more dubious concept of genius. But it is useful, nevertheless, indeed indispensable. Without it architecture would lose the special relationship to history from which it draws its cultural and critical depth.

CHAPTER 8
THE CITY

Cities endure for hundreds, even thousands of years. Rome was founded, according to tradition, in 753 BC and not only does it still exist but it is still alive, functioning as well, or as badly, as it ever did. Ancient Romans, if brought back to life in the twenty-first century, would probably be appalled and terrified by the modern city. But once they had got over the shock they would begin to recognize parts of it, not just the preserved ruins of the Forum or the Palatine Hill, but the ordinary streets, their directions and connections, their relationship to the seven hills and to the old roads leading out of Rome. Cities have a special relationship to time and to human memory. In a sense, a city is a man-made object, but its complexity and the depth of its history make it more like something natural – its streets, squares and landmarks like rivers, forests and hills. We can dam the rivers, raze the forests and level the hills but not without a sense of loss because we are destroying our own past, both private and collective, a past that restricts but also nourishes our lives. Cities are 'monumental' not in the sense of grand or imposing, like a temple or a town hall, but in the sense that they embody memories and associations. The word 'monumental' comes from the Latin *monere* which means to remind or warn. Cities remind us of our own personal histories and of the history of the society we live in. They remind us who we are.

Few of the buildings that line the Edgware Road in London are more than about 150 years old but the street itself is much older; the Romans called it Watling Street. So the Roman street survives not as a material, but as a virtual presence – a line, a direction, a human habit. It is surprising how many of these ancient virtual presences survive in European cities, even when they have no obvious modern function. We think of the Piazza Navona in Rome as a Baroque space, dominated as it is by Bernini's Fountain of the Four Rivers and by Borromini's Church of St Agnese. But why is the piazza so long and narrow? Because there has been a long, narrow open space here since ancient times, when it

An ancient Roman time traveller would no doubt be horrified by the Rome of today, but once he had recovered from the shock he would begin to recognize certain features of the city he knew – certain roads, monumental buildings and open spaces. Cities endure. They are the collective memory of a society and they give it stability and continuity. This is what the word 'monumental' really means.

was called the Stadium of Domitian and used to stage chariot races and other bloodthirsty public spectacles. There are similar survivals in almost every old Italian city. Walk in the narrow streets of Florence just west of the Piazza Santa Croce, and you will come across a curious curving street called the Via di Bentaccordi which traces the outline of a vanished Roman amphitheatre. In nearby Lucca, the form of the old amphitheatre is even better preserved, and here its presence is acknowledged in the name of the Piazza Anfiteatro, now the main public open space of the city. The standardized plan of a Roman castrum or military camp, with its Cardo (north–south oriented street) and Decumanus (east–west oriented street) forming a crossroads in the centre, is still clearly discernible in the current street maps of cities all over Europe and the Middle East.

In cities, individual buildings are frequently demolished and replaced but the streets and public open spaces tend to stay put. We could think of the city as a kind of matrix of virtual structures, renewing themselves on different time scales. First comes the street plan, ancient and relatively permanent, altered only in exceptional circumstances, like the carving of boulevards through the narrow streets of nineteenth century Paris by Baron Haussmann; then come the buildings, some long-lasting and monumental, some, like the London office blocks of the 1960s, overtaken by institutional and technological change and demolished after only 30 years or so; then come the interiors of the buildings, especially commercial buildings like offices and shops, which might be refitted every five or ten years; and so on down the time scale – the furniture in the houses, the goods in the shops, the news placards on the pavement that change every day.

Cities change in different ways in different cultures. In European cities, the pattern of land ownership is usually rather fluid. Small plots on which houses originally stood are often amalgamated to accommodate larger developments – office blocks, hotels, shopping centres, royal palaces. But in Japan, customs and laws governing inheritance tend to preserve the old site boundaries which means that

The Piazza Anfiteatro in Lucca is so called because it was the amphitheatre of the old Roman town. The oval plan-form survives. Around the perimeter, some fragments of Roman wall have been incorporated into the everyday residential and commercial buildings that now define the space.

Different cultures produce different urban forms. The strange profile of this street in Tokyo arises from land-owning customs which tend to preserve small building plots. It is said that the physical substance of Tokyo is reviewed completely about every 20 years.

This canyon-like street in Naples is typical of traditional European urban form. Spaces like streets, squares and courtyards seem to have been carved out of a solid mass of buildings. There are no doubts here about ownership or rights of way. The street is an unambiguously public space.

the only way buildings can grow is upwards. To European eyes, this gives the typical Tokyo street a curiously squashed appearance, its tall, thin buildings crowding together, the newer, taller ones dwarfing their older immediate neighbours. The history of the street is written in the profile of its buildings, as in a graph or histogram.

The physical forms of cities are endlessly varied to accommodate natural features like hills and rivers, as well as social and cultural forces that are more difficult to define. But they are also to some extent standardized. A city is usually a network of standard spatial elements: streets, squares, parks, yards, private gardens. In old European cities, these spaces tend to be very clearly defined, like the narrow streets in the centre of Rome or Naples, which are sliced like ravines through the living rock of the buildings that tower over them. These streets are unambiguously public. In a sense, because they are continuous, they constitute a single public space. There are no grey areas, no front gardens or grass verges such as you might find out in the suburbs. The streets belong to everybody and when they open out at a crossroads or in front of a church, the resulting piazza is like a public room, the facades of the surrounding buildings its decorated walls, the fountains, trees and benches its furniture. Occasionally as we wander through the city we might glimpse, through an archway, a little yard which is obviously not a public space. It belongs to the people that live or work in the buildings that enclose it and we probably shouldn't enter it unless we have some business with those people.

Traditional urban forms

This spatial and social clarity is characteristic of traditional cities. As tourists and sightseers we love the winding streets which are the result of a gradual adaptation over centuries to the comings and goings of daily life and the scale of the human figure. But perhaps it is their clarity rather than their picturesqueness that is most important. We tend to contrast them with the grid-iron plans of modern cities like New York or Chicago, but in fact grid-iron plans are nothing new. The medieval bastide towns of southern France, like Aigues Mortes in the Camargue; the Roman military settlements which lie just under the surface of cities like Florence or London; the Mediterranean Greek colonies of the fifth century BC; the camps that housed the workmen that built the pyramids of Egypt: all had grid-iron plans. Manhattan may have not have many narrow winding streets, but it does have that clear-cut quality, that unambiguous relationship between street and building, between public and private space, and to that extent, despite its skyscrapers, it is a traditional city.

Urban theorists of the last half century have been very interested in the clarity of traditional urban forms. One of their favourite illustrations is the extraordinarily detailed and accurate map of Rome created in the eighteenth century by the architect Giambattista Nolli.[1] Nolli's map represents buildings, or rather urban blocks, as dark masses against the white background of the streets and piazzas – a 'figure-ground' technique that has since been adopted as an analytical tool. Interestingly, the detailed interiors of churches, complete with columns, niches, and side chapels, are shown in white, because, as public spaces, they are

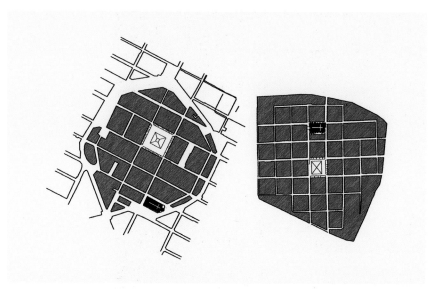

regarded as notionally external. Satellite photographs of Rome confirm the accuracy of the map, which, since the centre of the city has changed very little over the last 300 years, still serves well as a navigational aid for the tourist.

Nolli's map is important to urban theorists because it has become a critical 'counter example' to the practice of Modernist architects and urban planners who largely rejected traditional urban form in the early twentieth century. Modernists saw the city not as history written in stone but simply as a design project. The Modernist city was different from the traditional city in at least three important ways: it was a collection of separate buildings standing in open space rather than a solid mass from which open space was carved; it sorted its human uses or functions – home, work, leisure and so on – into separate zones rather than allowing them to mix together; and it was designed all at once as a perfect final product rather than the beginning of an open-ended process. The best example is not a real city but a visionary project, Le Corbusier's Ville Contemporaine, a city for three million people, designed in 1922.[2] It is, in a sense, a fiction, an unattainable Utopian ideal, but it is nevertheless worked out in some detail and it had an enormous influence on subsequent real urban developments. A central business district, consisting of 24 sixty-storey skyscrapers, is surrounded by luxury apartment blocks for a professional and administrative elite. Further out are the estates for the workers, and on the edge of town, the industrial zone.

It is easy to see how the sunny openness of the Ville Contemporaine – a city built in a park – would shine as a vision of the future at a time when the narrow, winding streets that tourists now find so picturesque were squalid slums. But there were deeper, architectural reasons why a Modernist architect would want to blow apart the dense, congealed mass of the traditional city. The new doctrine of functionalism demanded openness. If spaces were to be related optimally to one another, if healthy sunlight and fresh air were to be welcomed into buildings, if the load-bearing walls and pitched roofs of

The Nolli plan of Rome is a remarkably accurate plan of the city as it was in the eighteenth century. Because the city has changed so little, it can still be used as a tourist guide. Note how the plans of churches and other public buildings are shown in white, as if they were external spaces.

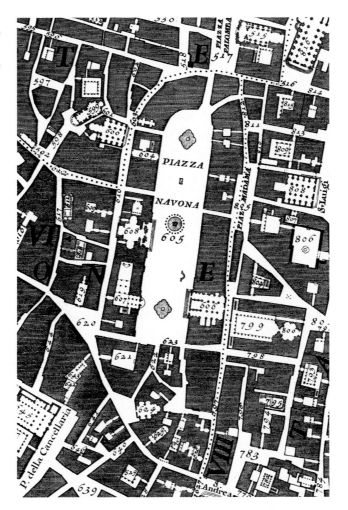

Le Corbusier's Ville Contemporaine is a visionary project for a city of three million inhabitants. This is the 'city of prophecy' as opposed to the 'city of memory'. Designed all at once as a perfect, Utopian solution, it cuts itself off from both the past and future. When we have built Utopia, what shall we do next?

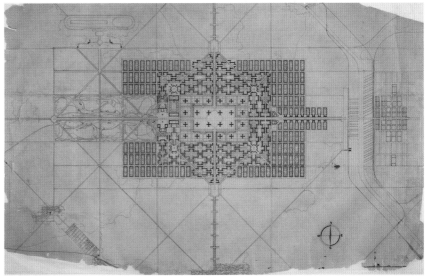

Le Corbusier's Plan Voisin, sponsored by a car manufacturer, proposed to flatten the Marais district of central Paris – the part that tourists now love best – to make way for a grid of 60-storey skyscrapers.

the old construction technology were to be flung off and replaced by the reinforced concrete frame and the free plan, then the new functional buildings would need room to breathe. The ideal Modernist building was a free-standing pavilion, like the one-off Purist houses that Le Corbusier was just beginning to design for his wealthy clients in 1922. It was unrealistic to design such houses for ordinary people, but row houses and apartment blocks could benefit from the same radical rethink provided they were not imprisoned in the slowly changing matrix of the traditional city. The old city must, if necessary, be destroyed to make way for the new. In 1925 Le Corbusier exhibited another visionary urban project called the Plan Voisin, not a complete new city this time but a new urban quarter in the middle of Paris. To accommodate it, the old district known as the Marais – the part that tourists now love the best – would have been razed to the ground.

Forty years later, when Le Corbusier's vision had been partly realized in high-rise estates all over the world, architects and urban theorists began to regret the passing of the traditional city and to appreciate its virtues. The city built in a park had turned out, in reality, to be a city built in a formless, meaningless open space. Was it public, or communal, or private? How could one tell? The tight correspondence between urban and social forms in the traditional city had been destroyed and the result was dissipation and neglect. Architects began to crave once again the clarity and containment of the street and the piazza. It seemed so much more human, not just in its scale and proportion but in the way it was used, the way that it brought together the activities of daily life rather than separating them into different zones. The Ville Contemporaine was like a diagram that illustrated, and reinforced, the fragmentation of modern life. A revival of traditional urban form might re-unite the fragments and heal the damaged wholeness.

In an influential book called *Collage City*, published in 1979, Colin Rowe and Fred Koetter contrasted the Modernist 'city of prophecy' with the traditional 'city of memory'.[3] In the city of prophecy the flow of time is frozen in a utopian vision, impossible to achieve in practice. The Ville Contemporaine is a pure invention, a uniform, abstract solution to a problem formulated in purely functional terms. Tradition plays no part

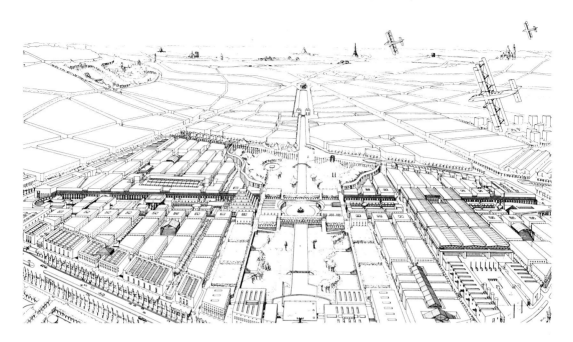

Léon Krier's 1976 project for a new urban quarter at La Villette in Paris looks at first like one of Le Corbusier's visionary projects of the 1920s and is even drawn in a similar style. On closer inspection, however, it turns out to be a restatement of the virtues of traditional, monumental urban form.

in it except as an obstacle to be overcome. It is cut off from the past like a person with no memory. And, being perfect, it is unalterable and therefore also cut off from the future. No work of change or improvement can take place without spoiling it. Like some disturbing vision of heaven, it has nothing left to do but sing its own praises for ever. All Utopias share this fundamental flaw: when we have built Utopia and thrown a big party to celebrate our achievement, we still have to get up the next morning and live our lives. But what life is there left to live? In the traditional city, the city of memory, there is no final, perfect state, only a continuum that remembers the past but is open to the future. The buildings may be demolished and rebuilt, but the streets remain.

Paradoxically, the revived appreciation of the traditional city in the 1960s and 70s also took the form of visionary projects, such as Léon Krier's proposal for the redevelopment of the La Villette quarter of northern Paris, published in 1976. With its grid-iron plan and flat-roofed buildings, at first it looks every bit as mechanistic as the Ville Contemporaine, but it also has that clear-cut quality, that emphasis on defined and contained space, that we saw in the Nolli map of Rome. And we can imagine how it might change. The buildings themselves are represented almost diagrammatically, as if they are merely place holders for future, more detailed designs. In the real world, the effect of this revival of interest in the traditional city was necessarily more fragmentary, but we can see it clearly in the recent history of sensitive city-centre sites like Paternoster Square next to St Paul's Cathedral in London. The old medieval quarter was destroyed by bombing in 1940 and replaced in the early 1960s by a typical Modernist scheme, much admired at the time, with office buildings, including a 16-storey tower, arranged freely on a pedestrian deck over an underground car park. By the 1980s,

the buildings were out of date and unloved and a long argument ensued about the best way to replace them. This finally resulted in a thoroughly traditional plan, with pedestrian streets and squares clearly defined by big office buildings in vaguely classical styles with shops on the ground floor. The overall effect is rather bland and hardly to be compared with old Italian precedents, but the substitution of Modernism by a version of traditional urban space is clear enough.

The motorized city

Time, then, is the key to understanding traditional and Modernist urban form. But there is another factor, related to time, that is perhaps even more important: speed. When everything in the city moved at the pace of human or animal locomotion, the streets were shaped and scaled in proportion to this pace. The coming of the motor car changed all that. It isn't just a question of traffic – there were traffic jams in ancient Rome – it is a question of the speed of the traffic, or rather its potential speed. It is said that the traffic in central London moves no faster now than it did a hundred years ago, but the fact that motor vehicles have the potential to travel must faster has opened up the possibility of a different kind of urban form.

The tight-packed traditional centres of European cities are resistant to the transforming effect of potential speed precisely because of their

Paternoster Square, on the north side of St Paul's Cathedral in London, was rebuilt after the Second World War in typical modernist style, but when it was rebuilt again in the 1990s traditional urban form, with contained streets and squares, reasserted itself. The effect is inoffensive, but rather bland.

enduring, monumental nature. But on the outskirts it's different, and in a twentieth-century megalopolis like Los Angeles, which covers an area of 1,295 square kilometres (500 square miles), the motor car has almost completely erased any remnants of traditional urban form. Poor people still travel around Lost Angeles at ground level on public buses that move relatively slowly. There is still some possibility of living and working in a neighbourhood, and even of walking a couple of blocks to a mini-mall. But above these shabby, formless streets is a faster city of elevated freeways on which richer people move at speed between the parking lots of the mainly commercial premises that substitute for traditional public space, and nobody ever walks anywhere. In this Los Angeles, traditional urban form is irrelevant because proximity has been replaced by speed. The continuous spatial experience of walking in the city, with all its potential for chance encounters, has been superseded by a sequence of spatial episodes – the home, the office, the shop, the restaurant – separated by short doses of that peculiar combination of cosiness and danger that is car travel. The city has been exploded, or rather it has been built in a pre-exploded condition. In this setting, architecture has no monumental function and no responsibility to its neighbours. What does it matter if the shopping mall and the cinema complex and the fast food outlet are all built in different styles? They are never experienced together anyway. They are isolated pockets of architectural invention with no context – temporal or spatial – to give them meaning.

Continuity and scale are key concepts. It seems almost absurd to compare a city like Los Angeles with a city like Venice (Venice, Italy, that is). They might almost be on different planets. But the contrast is instructive. There are no wheeled motor vehicles in Venice. Its isolated position in the lagoon and the canals that are its main streets allow only slow moving 'vehicles' like gondolas, vaporettos and barges. All very picturesque. But the important thing is the effect that this slowness has had on the form of the city, preserving intact its pre-industrial character (if only for consumption by the tourist industry, but that's another matter). Each neighbourhood, with its canals, its streets, its church, and its piazza (not just a public gathering place but also a rainwater collector discharging into the ornate well at its centre that is the symbolic focus of the everyday life) is scaled appropriately for the community it accommodates. The controlling factor is the normal speed of travel, which is walking pace. How long it takes to walk from the edge of the neighbourhood to the centre is the measure that creates that neighbourhood. Speed regulates the scale and proximity of essential facilities like churches, piazzas and wells and thereby creates urban form – the heights of buildings, the widths of streets, the density of occupation, and so on. Why do tourists love Venice so much? Because the enforced absence of wheeled motor vehicles has preserved its slowness, which in turn has preserved its fundamentally human quality. The individual buildings of Venice are stylistically rather diverse – Byzantine, Gothic, Renaissance-classical – but together they create a coherent form that is itself a kind of communal or collective architecture, assembled gradually over the centuries. It is what the Italian architect and urban theorist Also Rossi called, in the title of his most important book, 'the architecture of the city'. Any addition to this architecture must win its

Is the Los Angeles freeway an urban or an anti-urban form? The architectural historian Rayner Banham said that driving on the freeways was 'a special way of being alive'. Below the flyovers, however, lies another city in which poor people travel by bus and there is still some possibility of living in a neighbourhood and walking along the streets.

Venice (Italy) is the opposite of Los Angeles. It is a slow city, and the absence of motor vehicles has preserved a scale and density created by the pace of walking and of water travel. The basic components of the city – piazzas, canals, streets, buildings, bridges, ancient wells – are all related to each other in a spatial continuity (which attracts thousands of tourists, but that is another story).

place by agreeing not to spoil it. This is the opposite of Los Angeles. In Venice no one would dare to ignore the spatial and temporal context of the city. In recent years, almost no one has dared to build in Venice at all.

If Venice has a fundamentally human quality, does this mean that motorized cities like Los Angeles are fundamentally inhuman? Not necessarily. They too have their apologists and appreciators. The architectural historian Reyner Banham, for example, was a connoisseur of the LA freeways and the dispersed urban environment they produced. He called it 'Autopia'.[4] Driving on the freeways, he said, was 'a special way of being alive'. In their 1972 book, *Learning from Las Vegas*, Robert Venturi, Denise Scott Brown and Steven Izenour reveal their secret love of the motorized American city, and in particular of one of its most important components, the roadside commercial strip. Gas stations, fast food outlets, motels and supermarkets don't usually count as proper architecture. Respectable critics and commentators either ignore them or defame them as a form of pollution. Peter Blake wrote a book about the roadsides of America called *God's Own Junkyard*.[5] But for Venturi a gas station is just as interesting as a Venetian palace and a lot more relevant to everyday American experience. He constructs a theory of roadside architecture just as Aldo Rossi constructed a theory of the traditional European city, using similar concepts and language. Casinos are compared to cathedrals, parking lots to the gardens of Versailles, and the sprawl of the strip is contrasted with the containment of the Roman piazza. The Nolli map of Rome is mentioned.

But perhaps Venturi's most important insight is that the key determinants of this twentieth century urban form are speed and communication. Put very simply, this is a landscape of objects in space, strung out along a road, and the distance between those objects is fixed by the speed of the passing vehicles. Each object, or building, must attract the attention of the driver and persuade him or her to pull in. The crucial part of the architecture is therefore the sign that lets you know what goods or services are on offer in the building, from a hamburger to an instant wedding. The design of the functional part of the building is less important. It can be simple and cheap, even if it's a wedding chapel. The building becomes, in Venturi's terminology, a 'decorated shed'. And this is not seen as a bad thing. There is a long architectural tradition of decorated sheds. A medieval cathedral is, conceptually at least, a kind of decorated shed. Its west front is like a big, composite sign conveying, through representations of biblical figures, saints, devils and monsters, a complex message about the spiritual merchandise in which the building deals. This kind of far-fetched comparison is typical of Venturi's provocative style, but it has a grain of truth and its critical force is greatest when turned on what he perceives as the sullen dumbness of orthodox Modernist architecture. The decorated shed is celebrated as a practical, vernacular, characteristically American form that has its origins in the simple wooden buildings of the old frontier towns, the saloons and sheriffs' offices with their flat facades, taller than the buildings they fronted, defining a rudimentary street. It is a form peculiarly well suited to the strung out, motorized city, but with one modification: the facade has to be detached from its building and turned through 90 degrees to face the oncoming traffic. It becomes a 'totem', conveying its message partly symbolically but mainly straightforwardly in written language – the brand, the prices, the special offers, the valet parking. The building itself is now just a plain shed. Inside, it may be fitted out as a utilitarian retail outlet or as a luxurious restaurant, but no one notices the outside. By the time it comes into view, the driver's attention has already been distracted by the next big totem along the road.

Digital technology, distance and time

Technology changes cities, as the example of the motor car demonstrates. Digital technology might yet have an even more profound effect on urban form. In the modern world, distance has almost been abolished and proximity is no longer an important factor in many human transactions. We shouldn't exaggerate the power of digital communication technologies. The change they bring is mainly one of degree rather than of kind – an email is only a faster letter. And there is nothing new about virtual worlds; a novel is a virtual world. Nevertheless, we seem to be experiencing a collapsing of space and a dissolving of matter, including even, in a strange way, the matter of our own bodies. In the dealings of everyday life, the physical presence of the people we know, the people we work with, even the people we love, is not essential most of the time. We can always email them, call them on the mobile or follow them on Twitter to find out what they are up to. We can meet them in a video conference or in an imaginary place, like the popular virtual world known as Second Life. We can meet strangers there too, though we won't necessarily see them as who they really are. They might have chosen to be someone else when they concocted the avatar that represents them. The very identity of individual human beings is becoming uncertain. But then when was it ever certain?

Cities deal in physicality and proximity. They are like machines for facilitating physical meetings. Or perhaps they are markets in which the price of proximity is fixed. Until very recently, people who worked had to be near one another, in the factory or the office, the shop or the school. Space had to be found for various activities, it had to be located near other spaces that accommodated related activities, and there had to be physical links between them. A shop on its own in the middle of a field would do no business but in a street with other shops it becomes a place worth visiting. This economy of proximity was defined by physical boundaries and shared passageways – buildings and streets, figure and ground. Now all that is becoming irrelevant. We no longer have to stroll down to the town square to buy provisions in the market and hear the news and gossip; we can order what we need online and switch on the television for continuous bulletins. So what role is left for the town square? We don't need it any more. And soon we won't need the business district or the shopping centre either. Mechanized industry and the motor car began the destruction of the city; digital communication is finishing the job.

The French philosopher Paul Virilio describes how, in the nineteenth-century industrial city, time began to take precedence over space as the organizing principle of urban life.[6] Work, defined as a period of time – the three shifts per day of the factory or the nine-to-five of the office – became life's city centre, while leisure time and vacations became its suburbs. Conversely, the functional patchwork of the modern city, with its business district, industrial zones and residential suburbs, was the spatial reflection of a temporal reality. Space and time collided violently twice a day in the rush hour. But now, in the digital age, time no longer rules. Simultaneity is the new principle. Even the natural differentiation of day and night has been cancelled by instant global communication. On the computer screen, as Virilio puts it, 'everything is always already present'. Robots man the factories and office work is shifting back into the home as broadband connectivity spreads. It no longer matters much when or where the human work is done.

What are the architectural consequences of this spatial and temporal convulsion? If space is the essence of architecture then the fundamentally non-spatial digital technologies must be seen as a threat to traditional architectural forms. Take the question of remote surveillance and its effect on that ancient and almost universal urban form, the street. The street has a number of obvious functions – a passageway for through traffic, a corridor linking adjacent properties, a gallery for the display of goods in shop windows – but it also has the less obvious function of preventing crime. As everybody knows, crime usually takes place in dark alleyways and other sparsely populated urban spaces that nobody supervises. In the busy street you are safe because any crime is bound to be witnessed and muggers are therefore deterred. Even at night, when the shoppers and revellers have gone home, the street will be relatively safe provided there are windows facing it from which residents just might be keeping watch. This is old-style surveillance, which relies for its effectiveness on the physical shaping of space – that is to say architecture. But now the word surveillance means CCTV cameras sprinkled liberally over the whole city and connected to banks of screens monitored by persons of uncertain status in secret locations. Note the spatial displacement that has occurred. The visible, physical presence of a policeman in a particular place has been supplanted by the hidden, virtual presence of a security person in a dozen places at once. Whatever we think of the civil liberties aspect of this, it must eventually have a corrosive effect on urban space in general and on traditional streets in particular. Why do you need a street if you have CCTV? In theory, buildings and building entrances could be arranged randomly – scattered over a 'campus' perhaps – provided there is good lighting and blanket camera coverage. In theory, the certain knowledge of the presence of the cameras will deter criminals and reassure everyone else that they are safe. But will it feel safe? Does feeling safe depend on mere knowledge or is it more a question of spatial instinct? Does it rely on the physical presence and vulnerability of the body? These are important questions for architects.

Surveillance is just one example of the way that a digital technology tends to undermine the organized physicality of the city. The relationship between form and function in urban architecture is far from straightforward but when we add in the digital effect the situation becomes even more fluid. Functional building types don't just become unstable, they dissolve completely into that radically un-spatial realm that we used to call 'cyberspace'. The internet is a kind of city, a city in which physicality and proximity are irrelevant. The complete repertoire of public building types – those monumental anchor points of the traditional city – is represented in the convenient, searchable, space-less simultaneity of the internet: libraries, museums, town halls, banks, stock exchanges, schools, universities, shopping centres. (Concert halls, theatres, cinemas and sports arenas were forced long ago to share the uniqueness of the experience they offer with radio and television and their related recording technologies.) How long can the city hold out against this virtual competitive onslaught? Will urban architecture – the systematic organization of physical space and proximity – eventually disappear both as an art and as a shared experience?

Well, probably not, for one simple reason. People, for the foreseeable future at least, are embodied beings. We live in our bodies and there is nowhere else we can live. Bodies are physical and they need real, extended space in which to be. They also have to be protected from the sometimes hostile environmental conditions that prevail on this planet – the weather, in other words. That's why we used to live in caves and now build artificial caves. Artificial sheltering structures, because they are human products, immediately and inevitably become cultural as well as practical and architecture is born. Most architects love digital technologies and are quick to adopt them in their day to day practice. Some become besotted with them and begin to imagine that they represent a new kind of architecture dealing with a new kind of space. If there is such a thing as 'cyberspace', the argument goes, then it must need organizing, and who better to do this than people that are trained in the organization of space? The 'paper architecture' of the past – all those visionary projects like the Ville Contemporaine – has become the digital architecture of the present. But this, surely, is a misunderstanding. The 'space' that we seem to see in the computer is an illusion, like the space in a Renaissance perspective painting. It beguiles the mind but it is useless to the body. Architecture, we might argue, is not the ally, but the enemy of virtual space. Architecture represents that embodiment and situatedness – that 'being there' – that is the foundation of all human experience, including the experience of the virtual.

Architecture and the virtual world

A simple example might clarify this. It is ironic that while the real, physical city is being displaced and distorted by digital technology, the virtual worlds of the internet are full of images of physical architecture. In Second Life, people are busy choosing identities for themselves, meeting people, running businesses, buying and selling things, learning languages, and attending art galleries and concerts, just like in the real world. You can of course do all of these things elsewhere on the internet but Second Life is more appealing because it is, or seems to be, unified and continuous. You don't have to switch between web-sites to get from the language school to the art gallery, you can, in theory at least, 'travel' from one to the other through something that is almost like space. Actually, you can 'teleport' yourself from place to place, which is more of less the same thing as typing in another web address, but the illusion is maintained that you are still in the same 'world'. How is the illusion maintained? By furnishing the virtual world with representations of at least some of the physical features of the real world. So there is land and sea and sky, they are where you would expect to find them – the sky is up, the land is down – and they are appropriately coloured and textured. You can almost believe that plants would grow in the ground and that rain might fall from the sky. Your avatar stands on the ground and is subject to a force that is rather similar to gravity. There is light to see by and it presumably comes from some kind of sun or moon, for there is day and night, and they alternate on the same 24-hour cycle as the real day and night. This isn't just a picture or a film because we ourselves seem to be able to move around in it. You could say that it is just a video game, but the fact that there are no rules or goals or levels, and the fact that anyone can join in, seems to change its status, persuading us to accept it as an actual, if not a real, world. For some people it is real enough to inhabit for long periods of time, real enough to make a living in, real enough to get married in and build a home.

In Second Life nobody really needs architecture. There is no wind and rain to exclude, no gravity to resist, no bodily human presence and therefore no need for physical comfort. Yet Second Life contains many buildings. While the cities of the real world are under threat from non-spatial digital technologies, in the virtual world, people still cling to a semblance of physical architecture.

What might this home look like? How will it be designed? What factors should the Second Life architect take into account? Will they be the same as those for a house in the real world: local climate, availability of suitable building materials, water supply and drainage, energy efficiency, subsoil conditions? No. The architect can safely ignore all of these factors because this is only going to be a pretend home, like a home in fairy story. The walls will not need to be insulated because there is no warm air to contain or cold air to exclude; in fact the walls don't need to be there at all, unless to preserve the privacy of the avatars that 'live' in the house. No need for a roof either, since it never rains and the heat of the sun can't actually be felt. Structure? Again, no need, for there is no gravity. It turns out that the force that keeps things on the virtual ground can be switched off. Everybody in Second Life can hover or fly at will.

The truth is that it just isn't necessary to build buildings in Second Life, so why do so many people do it? And why do those buildings look like real buildings, with walls and roofs and floors and chimneys and porches? For the same reason that this virtual world has a ground and a sky: because this is an environment designed for humans and humans can't live, even virtually, in abstract space. They must feel the resistance of the real world, the resistance that defines life. In a world where the primary conditions for the existence of things seem to have been abolished, those conditions must be recreated in some form of representation. So, paradoxically, while the cities of the real world are being threatened by the space-dissolving forces of digital technology, the cities of the internet are desperately clinging to physical, spatial, enduring, human architecture.

INDEX

Page numbers in *italics* refer to picture captions

FOOTNOTES

Introduction

1. One of the more interesting and ambitious books on the design process was *Notes on the Synthesis of Form* by Christopher Alexander (Harvard University Press, 1964). Alexander went on to write several more influential books about architectural theory, including *A Pattern Language* (Oxford University Press, 1977) and *A Timeless Way of Building* (Oxford University Press, 1979).

2. The first British postgraduate course in History and Theory of Architecture was founded at the University of Essex in 1968 by Joseph Rykwert, assisted by Dalibor Vesely. At about the same time, the Institute of Architectural and Urban Studies (IAUS) in New York was forging links with the architecture schools at Princeton, Columbia and Yale. See: 'Invention in the Shadow of History: Joseph Rykwert at the University of Essex' by Helen Thomas in *Journal of Architectural Education*, vol. 58, no. 2, November 2004, pp.39–45.

3. The Thinkers for Architects series is published by Taylor & Francis.

4. Andrea Kahn, 'Representations and Misrepresentations: On Architectural Theory', in *Journal of Architectural Education*, vol. 47, no. 3, February 1994, p.162.

Chapter 1

1. Dalibor Vesely, *Architecture in the Age of Divided Representation: The Question of Creativity in the Shadow of Production*, MIT Press, 2004, p.4.

2. 'Elgin Marbles' in *The Oxford Dictionary of Art*, ed. Ian Chilvers, Oxford University Press, 2004; http://www.enotes.com/oxford-art-encyclopedia/elgin-marbles

3. See: Le Corbusier, *Towards a New Architecture*, Dover Publications, 1986, Chapter III.

4. '...that which withers in the age of mechanical reproduction is the aura of the work of art.' Quotation from 'The Work of Art in the Age of Mechanical Reproduction' in *Illuminations: Walter Benjamin*, Hannah Arendt, ed., Fontana, 1992, p.223.

5. Oliver Sacks, *The Man Who Mistook his Wife for a Hat, and Other Clinical Tales*, Picador, 2007 (reprint), p.10

6. ibid., p.13

Chapter 2

1. John Summerson, *The Classical Language of Architecture*, Thames & Hudson, 1980.

2. Charles Jencks, *The Language of Post-modern Architecture*, Academy Editions, 1991.

3. W. Shakespeare, *The Merchant of Venice*, Act V, Scene 1.

4. See: James K. Feibleman, *An Introduction to Peirce's Philosophy*, Allen and Unwin, 1960.

5. See: Jacques Derrida, *Of Grammatology*, Johns Hopkins University Press, 1976.

6. Philip Johnson and Mark Wigley, *Deconstructivist Architecture*, The Museum of Modern Art/Little Brown and Company, 1988.

Chapter 3

1. The theory of forms occurs in many of Plato's dialogues. *Timaeus* contains a discussion of the cosmological and geometrical aspects of the topic.

2. See Aristotle's *Physics*, *Book Two*, for a discussion of the doctrine of the four causes.

3. Leon Battista Alberti, *The Ten Books of Architecture, The 1755 Leoni Edition*, Dover Publications, 1986, Book IX, Chapter V.

4. See: Samuel Y. Edgerton, Jr, *The Renaissance Rediscovery of Linear Perspective*, Basic Books, Inc., 1975.

5. See: Gropius's 1910 Memorandum to AEG on the factory production of houses, quoted in full in 'Gropius at Twenty Six' in *Architectural Review*, July 1961, pp.49–51.

6. See: Colin Davies, *The Prefabricated Home*, Reaktion Books, 2005, Chapter 6.

7. Le Corbusier, *The Modulor: A Harmonious Measure to the Human Scale Universally Applicable to Architecture and Mechanics*, Birkhauser, 2000, p.56.

Chapter 4

1. Gaston Bachelard, *The Poetics of Space*, John R. Stilgo, trans., Orion Press, 1964, p.18.

2. *Martin Heidegger: Basic Writings*, David Farrell Krell, ed., Routledge, 1993, Chapter VIII.

3. See 'Panopticism' in Michel Foucault, *Discipline and Punish*, A. Sheridan, trans., Penguin, 1977. Extract appears in *Rethinking Architecture*, N. Leach, ed., Routledge, 1997.

4. See: 'Talk at the conclusion of the Otterlo Congress (1959)' in *Louis Kahn: Essential Texts*, Robert Twombly, ed., Norton, 2003.

5. See: Victor Buchli, 'Moisei Ginzburg's Narkomfin Communal House in Moscow: Contesting the Social and Material World' in *Journal of the Society of Architectural Historians*, vol. 57, no. 2 (June 1998), pp.160–181.

Chapter 5

1. John Ruskin, *The Seven Lamps of Architecture*, Dover Publications reprint, 1989, p.35.

2. See: Colin Davies, *High Tech Architecture*, Thames & Hudson, 1988.

3. A. W. N. Pugin, *True Principles of Pointed or Christian Architecture*, Academy Editions reprint, 1973, p.2.

4. See: Marc-Antoine Laugier, *An Essay on Architecture*, W. and A. Herrmann, trans., Hennessey & Ingalls, 1977.

5. Gottfried Semper, *The Four Elements of Architecture and Other Writings*, H. F. Mallgrave and W. Herrmann, trans., Cambridge University Press, 1989, p.103.

6. John Summerson, *Heavenly Mansions and Other Essays*, Cresset Press, 1949.

7. John Ruskin, *Lectures on Architecture and Painting Delivered at Edinburgh in November 1853*, London, Smith Elder, 1855. Addenda to Lectures I and II, paragraph 66.

Chapter 6

1. See: *The Essential Frank Lloyd Wright: Critical Writings on Architecture*, Bruce Brooks Pfeiffer, ed., Princeton Architectural Press, 2008, p.56.

2. D'Arcy Wentworth Thompson, *On Growth and Form*, Cambridge University Press, 1961, p.16.

3. See: Manuel DeLanda, annotated bibliography at: http://www.cddc.vt.edu/host/delanda/

4. Gilles Deleuze, *Difference and Repetition*, Paul Patton, trans., Continuum, 1994, p.222.

5. See: James Roy Newman, *The World of Mathematics*, Volume I, Dover Publications, 2000, Chapter 4.

6. Manuel DeLanda, 'Deleuze and the Genesis of Form', in *Art Orbit*, no. 1, Stockholm: Art Node, March 1998.

7. See Manuel DeLanda, 'Materiality: Anexact and Intense', in *NOX: Machining Architecture*, Lars Spuybroek, ed., Thames & Hudson, 2004, pp.370–77.

8. ibid., p.374.

9. Manuel DeLanda, 'Deleuze and the Use of the Genetic Algorithm in Architecture' in *Designing for a Digital World*, Neil Leach, ed., Wiley, 2002, pp.117–120.

Chapter 7
1. See: Georg Wilhelm Friedrich Hegel, *The Philosophy of History*, J. Sibree, trans., Dover Publications, 1956.

2. Sigfried Giedion, *Space, Time and Architecture: The Growth of a New Tradition*, Oxford University Press, 1967, p.2.

3. ibid, p.5.

4. ibid, p.18.

5. Karl Popper, *The Poverty of Historicism*, Routledge & Kegan Paul, 1957, Preface.

6. Roland Barthes, 'The Death of the Author' in Stephen Heath, ed., *Image, Music, Text*, Fontana, 1984.

7. Marc Treib, *Space Calculated in Seconds: The Philips Pavilion, Le Corbusier, Edgard Varèse*, Princeton University Press, 1996.

8. See: *Le Corbusier: The Art of Architecture*, Alexander von Vegesack, ed., Vitra Design Museum, 2008.

Chapter 8
1. See: http://nolli.uoregon.edu/

2. See: Le Corbusier, *The City of Tomorrow and its Planning*, F. Etchells, trans., Architectural Press, 1971.

3. Colin Rowe and Fred Koetter, *Collage City*, MIT Press, 1978.

4. Rayner Banham, *Los Angeles: The Architecture of Four Ecologies*, Penguin Books, 1971, Chapter 11.

5. Peter Blake, *God's Own Junkyard: The Planned Deterioration of America's Landscape*, Henry Holt, 1979.

6. See: Paul Virilio, 'The Overexposed City' in *Rethinking Architecture*, Neil Leach, ed., Routledge, 1997

BIBLIOGRAPHY

Introduction
Alexander, C., *Notes on the Synthesis of Form*, Harvard University Press, 1964.

Banham, R., *Theory and Design in the First Machine Age*, Architectural Press, 1962 (2001 printing).

Braham, W., Hale, J., and Sadar, J., eds, *Rethinking Technology: A Reader in Architectural Theory*, Routledge, 2007.

Harbison, R., *Thirteen Ways: Theoretical Investigations in Architecture*, MIT Press, 1997.

Hays, K. M., ed., *Architecture Theory Since 1968*, MIT Press, 1998.

Jencks, C. and Kropf, K., eds, *Theories and Manifestoes of Contemporary Architecture*, Wiley-Academy, 2006.

Koolhaas, R., *Conversations with Students*, Sanford Kwinter, ed., Rice University School of Architecture, 1996.

Koolhaas, R., et al, *Small, Medium, Large, Extra-large*, 010 Publishers, 1995.

Kruft, H-W., *A History of Architectural Theory from Vitruvius to the Present*, Philip Wilson Ltd, 1994.

Leach, N., ed., *Rethinking Architecture: A Reader in Cultural Theory*, Routledge, 1997.

Le Corbusier, *Towards a New Architecture*, Dover Publications, 1986.

Mallgrave, H. F., ed., *Architectural Theory, Volume 1: An Anthology from Vitruvius to 1870*, Blackwell, 2005.

Mallgrave, H. F., and Contandriopoulos, C., eds, *Architectural Theory, Volume II: An Anthology from 1871 to 2005*, Blackwell, 2008.

Mallgrave, H. F., *Modern Architectural Theory: A Historical Survey 1673–1968*, Cambridge University Press, 2005.

Nesbitt, K., ed., *Theorizing a New Agenda for Architecture: An Anthology of Architectural Theory 1965–1995*, Princeton Architectural Press, 1996.

Tafuri, M., *Architecture and Utopia: Design and Capitalist Development*, MIT Press, 1976.

1 Representation
Benjamin, W., *Illuminations*, edited and with an introduction by H. Arendt, Fontana, 1992.

Hersey, G. L., *The Lost Meaning of Classical Architecture: Speculations on Ornament from Vitruvius to Venturi*, MIT Press, 1988

Pérez-Gómez, A., *Architectural Representation and the Perspective Hinge*, MIT Press, 1997.

Pevsner, N., *An Outline of European Architecture*, Penguin, 1963.

Sacks, O., *The Man Who Mistook his Wife for a Hat, and Other Clinical Tales*, Picador, 2007 (reprint).

Scruton, R., *The Aesthetics of Architecture*, Methuen, 1979.

Vesely, D., *Architecture in the Age of Divided Representation: The Question of Creativity in the Shadow of Production*, MIT Press, 2004.

Vitruvius, *On Architecture*, trans. R. Schofield, with an introduction by R. Tavernor, Penguin, 2009.

2 Language
Baudrillard, J., *Mass. Identity. Architecture: Architectural Writings of Jean Baudrillard*, F. Proto, ed., Wiley-Academy, 2003.

Broadbent, G., *Deconstruction: A Student Guide*, Academy Editions, 1991.

Derrida, J., *Of Grammatology*, Johns Hopkins University Press, 1976.

Derrida, J., and Eisenman, P., *Chora L Works*, J. Kipnis and T. Leeser, eds, Monacelli Press, 1997.

Eisenman, P., *Eisenman Inside Out: Selected Writings 1963–1988*, Yale University Press, 2004.

Eisenman, P., *Written Into the Void: Selected Writings 1990–2004*, Yale University Press, 2007.

Empson, W., *Seven Types of Ambiguity*, Pimlico, 2004.

Feibleman, J. K., *An Introduction to Peirce's Philosophy*, Allen and Unwin, 1960.

Hawkes, T., *Structuralism and Semiotics*, Methuen, 1977.

Jencks, C., *The Language of Post-Modern Architecture*, Academy Editions, 1991.

Jencks, C., *What is Post-Modernism?*, Academy Editions, 1996.

Jencks, C., and Baird, G., eds, *Meaning in Architecture*, Cresset Press, 1969.

Johnson, P., and Wigley, M., *Deconstructivist Architecture*, MoMA/Little Brown and Company, 1988.

Norris, C., *Deconstruction: Theory and Practice*, Methuen, 1982.

Norris, C., and Benjamin, A., *What is Deconstruction?*, Academy Editions, 1988.

Summerson, J., *The Classical Language of Architecture*, Thames & Hudson, 1980 (1996 printing).

Venturi, R., *Complexity and Contradiction in Architecture*, MoMA, 1977 (1998 printing).

Vidler, A., *The Architectural Uncanny: Essays in the Modern Unhomely*, MIT Press, 1992.

Wigley, M., *The Architecture of Deconstruction: Derrida's Haunt*, MIT Press, 1993.

3 Form
Alberti, Leon Battista, *The Ten Books of Architecture: The 1755 Leoni Edition*, Dover Publications, 1986.

Aristotle, *Physics, Books I and II*, William Charlton, trans., Oxford University Press, 1992.

Edgerton, S. Y., Jr, *The Renaissance Rediscovery of Linear Perspective*, Basic Books, Inc., 1975.

Evans, R., *The Projective Cast: Architecture and its Three Geometries*, MIT Press, 1995.

Evans, R., *Translations from Drawing to Building and Other Essays*, Architectural Association, 1997.

Le Corbusier, *The Modulor: A Harmonious Measure to the Human Scale Universally Applicable to Architecture and Mechanics*, Birkhauser, 2000.

Padovan, R., *Proportion: Science, Philosophy, Architecture*, Spon, 1999.

Plato, *Timaeus* and *Critias*, trans. D. Lee, Penguin Classics, 2008.

Rowe, C., *The Mathematics of the Ideal Villa and Other Essays*, MIT Press, 1976.

Scholfield, P. H., *The Theory of Proportion in Architecture*, Cambridge University Press, 1958.

Wittkower, R., *Brunelleschi and 'Proportion in Perspective'*, 1954

Wittkower, R., *Architectural Principles in the Age of Humanism*, Academy Editions, 1998.

4 Space
Bachelard, G., *The Poetics of Space*, Beacon Press, 1994.

Foucault, M., *Discipline and Punish*, trans. A. Sheridan, Penguin, 1977.

Heidegger, M., *Basic Writings*, D. F. Krell, ed., Routledge, 1993.

Heidegger, M., *Poetry, Language, Thought*, trans. A. Hofstadter, Harper and Row, 1975.

Kahn, L., *Louis Kahn: Essential Texts*, R. Twombly, ed., Norton, 2003.

Lefebvre, H., *The Production of Space*, trans. D. Nicholson-Smith, Blackwell, 1991.

Merleau-Ponty, M., *Basic Writings*, T. Baldwin, ed., Routledge, 2004.

Norberg-Schulz, C., *Meaning in Western Architecture*, Studio Vista, 1980 (1986 printing).

Norberg-Schulz, C., *Genius Loci: Towards a Phenomenology of Architecture*, Academy Editions, 1980.

Pallasmaa, J., *The Thinking Hand: Essential and Embodied Wisdom in Architecture*, Wiley, 2009.

Pevsner, N., *A History of Building Types*, Thames & Hudson, 1976.

Porphyrios, D., *Sources of Modern Eclecticism: Studies on Alvar Aalto*, Academy Editions, 1982.

Tschumi, B., *The Manhattan Transcripts*, Academy Editions, 1994.

Wertheim, M., *The Pearly Gates of Cyberspace*, Virago, 1999.

5 Truth
Bloomer, K., *The Nature of Ornament: Rhythm and Metamorphosis in Architecture*, Norton, 2000.

Brolin, B. C., *Architectural Ornament: Banishment and Return*, Norton, 2000.

Davies, C., *High Tech Architecture*, Rizzoli, 1988.

Davies, C., *Hopkins: The Work of Michael Hopkins and Partners*, Phaidon Press, 1993.

Frampton, K., *Studies in Tectonic Culture: The Poetics of Construction in Nineteenth and Twentieth Century Architecture*, J. Cava, ed., MIT Press, 1995.

Hardy, A., *Indian Temple Architecture: Form and Transformation*, Indira Gandhi National Centre for the Arts, 1995.

Laugier, M-A., *An Essay on Architecture*, trans. W. and A. Herrmann, Hennessey & Ingalls, 1977.

Loos, A., *Ornament and Crime: Selected Essays*, Ariadne Press, 1998.

Pugin, A. W. N., *The True Principles of Pointed or Christian Architecture*, Academy Editions, 1973 (reprint).

Ruskin, J., *Lectures on Architecture and Painting Delivered at Edinburgh in November 1853*, Smith Elder, 1855.

Ruskin, J., *The Seven Lamps of Architecture*, Dover Publications, 1989 (reprint).

Semper, G., *Style in the Technical and Tectonic Arts, or, Practical Aesthetics*, trans. H. F. Mallgrave and M. Robinson, Getty Research Institute, 2004.

Semper, G., *The Four Elements of Architecture and other Writings*, trans. H. F. Mallgrave and W. Herrmann, Cambridge University Press, 1989.

Summerson, J., *Heavenly Mansions and Other Essays on Architecture*, Cresset Press, 1949.

6 Nature
Balmond, C., *Element*, Prestel, 2007.

DeLanda, M., *Intensive Science and Virtual Philosophy*, Continuum, 2002.

Deleuze, G., *Difference and Repetition*, trans. P. Patton, Continuum, 1994.

Deleuze, G., *The Fold: Leibniz and the Baroque*, trans. T. Conley, Continuum, 2006.

Deleuze, G. and Guattari, F., *A Thousand Plateaus*, trans. B. Massumi, Athlone Press, 2004.

Fergusson, J., *An Historical Inquiry into the True Principles of Beauty in Art, More Especially with Reference to Architecture*, Longmans, Brown, Green and Longmans, 1849; paperback reprint Biblio Bazaar, 2010.

Leach, N., ed., *Designing for a Digital World*, Wiley-Academy, 2002.

Lynn, G., ed., *Folding in Architecture*, Wiley, 2004.

Panofsky, E., *Gothic Architecture and Scholasticism*, Archabbey Press, 1951.

Rudofsky, B., *Architecture without Architects: A Short Introduction to Non-pedigreed Architecture*, MoMA, 1964.

Simson, O. von, *The Gothic Cathedral: Origins of Gothic Architecture and the Medieval Concept of Order*, Routledge & Kegan Paul, 1962.

Spuybroek, L., ed., *NOX: Machining Architecture*, Thames & Hudson, 2004.

Steadman, P., *The Evolution of Designs: Biological Analogy in Architecture and the Applied Arts*, Routledge, 2008.

Terzidis, K., *Algorithmic Architecture*, Architectural Press, 2006.

Thompson, D. W., *On Growth and Form*, abridged edition J. T. Bonner, ed., Cambridge University Press, 1961.

Wright, F. L., *The Essential Frank Lloyd Wright: Critical Writings on Architecture*, B. B. Pfeiffer, ed., Princeton Architectural Press, 2008.

Zevi, B., *Towards an Organic Architecture*, Faber, 1950.

7 History
Anstey, T., Grillner, K., and Hughes, R., eds, *Architecture and Authorship*, Black Dog, 2007.

Barthes, R., *Barthes: Selected Writings*, introduced by S. Sontag, Fontana/Collins, 1983.

Barthes, R., *Image, Music, Text*, S. Heath, ed., Fontana, 1984.

Carr, E. H., *What is History?*, Penguin Books, 1964.

Davies, C., *Key Houses of the Twentieth Century: Plans, Sections and Elevations*, Laurence King, 2006.

Davies, C., *The Prefabricated Home*, Reaktion, 2005.

Frampton, K., *Labour, Work and Architecture: Collected Essays on Architecture and Design*, Phaidon Press, 2002.

Giedion, S., *Space, Time and Architecture: The Growth of a New Tradition*, Oxford University Press, 1967.

Hegel, G. W. F., *The Philosophy of History*, trans. J. Sibree, Dover Publications, 1956.

Kuhn, T. S., *The Structure of Scientific Revolutions*, University of Chicago Press, 1996.

Popper, K., *The Poverty of Historicism*, Routledge & Kegan Paul, 1957.

Treib, M., *Space Calculated in Seconds: The Philips Pavilion, Le Corbusier, Edgard Varèse*, Princeton University Press, 1996.

Watkin, D., *Morality and Architecture*, Clarendon Press, 1977.

Watkin, D., *Morality and Architecture Revisited*, John Murray, 2001.

Watkin, D., *The Rise of Architectural History*, Architectural Press, 1980.

8 The City
Augé, M., *Non-places: Introduction to an Anthropology of Supermodernity*, Verso, 1995.

Banham, R., *Los Angeles: The Architecture of Four Ecologies*, Penguin, 1971.

Benedikt, M., ed., *Cyberspace: First Steps*, MIT Press, 1992.

Blake, P., *God's Own Junkyard: The Planned Deterioration of America's Landscape*, Henry Holt, 1979.

Koolhaas, R., *Delirious New York: A Retroactive Manifesto for Manhattan*, 010 Publishers, 1994.

Krier, L., *Léon Krier: Architecture & Urban Design 1967–1992*, R. Economakis, ed., Academy Editions, 1992.

Le Corbusier, *The City of Tomorrow*, Architectural Press, 1971.

Mitchell, W. J., *City of Bits: Space, Place, and the Infobahn*, MIT Press, 1995.

Rossi, A., *The Architecture of the City*, MIT Press, 1982.

Rowe, C., and K., Fred, *Collage City*, MIT Press, 1978.

Sitte, C., *City Planning According to Artistic Principles*, trans. G. R. and C. Crasemann Collins, Phaidon, 1965.

Venturi, R., Scott Brown, D., and Izenour, S., *Learning from Las Vegas: The Forgotten Symbolism of Architectural Form*, MIT Press, 1977.